VENICE

Travel Guide 2025-2026

Itineraries, Local Tips, Must-See Attractions, Hidden Gems, and Practical Advice for Every Kind of Tourist

Jose S. Wulff

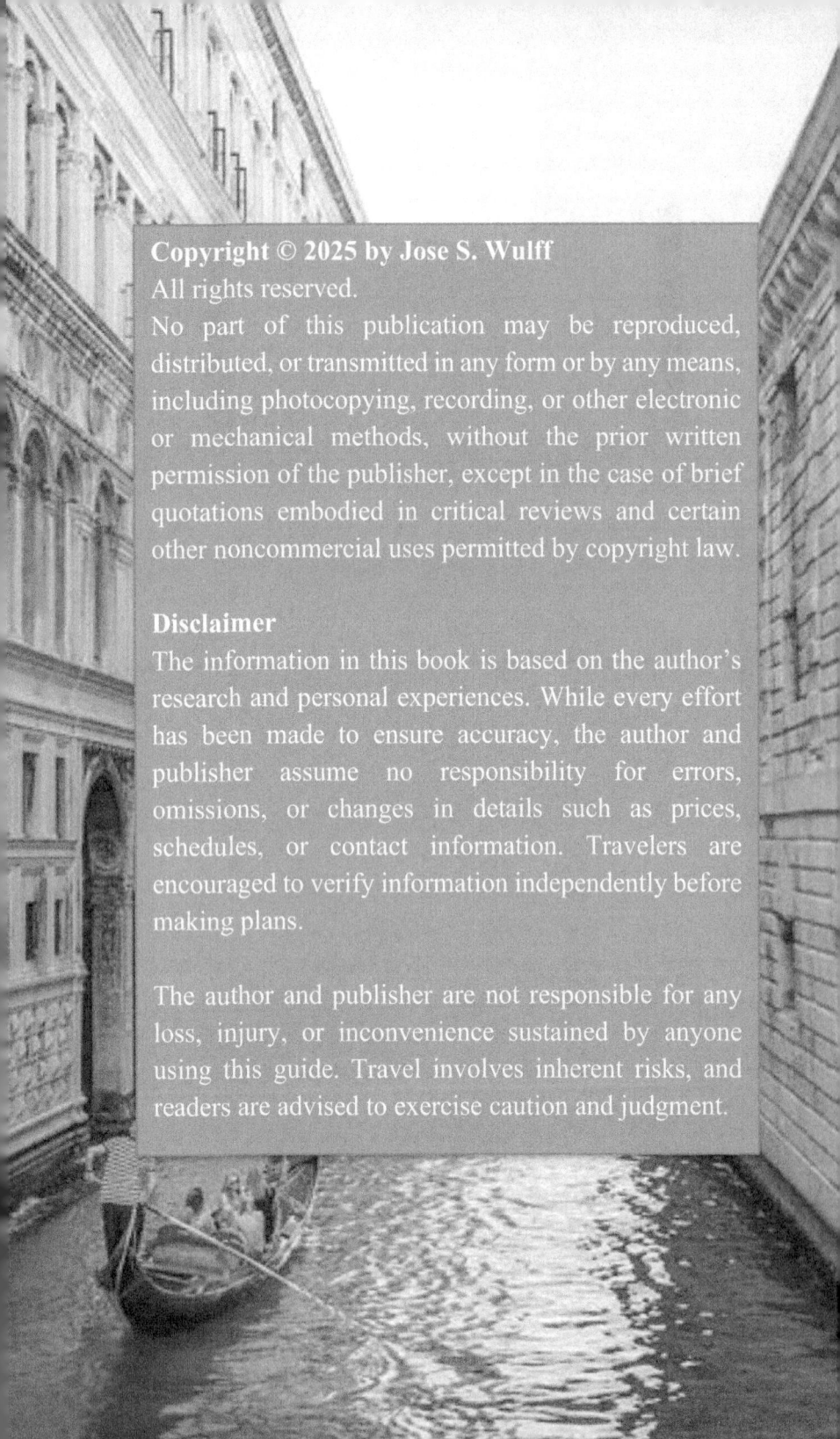

Copyright © 2025 by Jose S. Wulff
All rights reserved.
No part of this publication may be reproduced, distributed, or transmitted in any form or by any means, including photocopying, recording, or other electronic or mechanical methods, without the prior written permission of the publisher, except in the case of brief quotations embodied in critical reviews and certain other noncommercial uses permitted by copyright law.

Disclaimer

The information in this book is based on the author's research and personal experiences. While every effort has been made to ensure accuracy, the author and publisher assume no responsibility for errors, omissions, or changes in details such as prices, schedules, or contact information. Travelers are encouraged to verify information independently before making plans.

The author and publisher are not responsible for any loss, injury, or inconvenience sustained by anyone using this guide. Travel involves inherent risks, and readers are advised to exercise caution and judgment.

TABLE OF CONTENTS

TABLE OF CONTENTS 2

INTRODUCTION 6

THE REASON WHY VENICE IS AN ESSENTIAL TRAVEL DESTINATION 12

VENICE'S HISTORY 18

CHAPTER 1 22

ORGANIZING YOUR VACATION TO VENICE 22

    When to Go to Venice 22

    Examples of Itineraries 25

        Sample Itineraries for Three Days 25

        Sample Itineraries for Five Days 29

        Sample Itineraries for Seven Days 34

    Setting a Travel Budget 40

    Essentials for your Trip 44

        Things to Bring to Venice 44

CHAPTER 2 54

TRANSPORTATION OPTION FOR GETTING TO AND AROUND VENICE 54

    Reaching Venice 54

        By Air: Treviso and Marco Polo Airports 54

        By Train: Santa Lucia Station in Venice 58

    Getting Around the Lagoon 67

Gondolas, Vaporetto (Water Bus), and Water Taxis ... 67

Walking in Venice 71

Advice for a Stress-Free Arrival 76

CHAPTER 3 82

PLACES TO STAY IN VENICE 82

Selecting the Appropriate Neighborhood 82

San Marco: Venice's Center 82

Cannaregio: Genuine and Economical 86

Dorsoduro 91

Santa Croce, San Polo, and Castello 96

Accommodation Types 100

Luxurious Hotels 100

Charming B&Bs and Boutique Hotels 105

Low-Cost Apartments and Hostels 109

Tips for Booking 114

CHAPTER 4 119

THE FAMOUS ATTRACTIONS IN VENICE 119

Significant Landmarks 119

Piazza San Marco and St. Mark's Basilica 119

Doge's Palace with the Sighing Bridge 123

Grand Canal and Rialto Bridge 127

Hidden Gems and Off-the-Beaten-Path Spots 131

Acqua Alta Library 131

Calm Squares and Neighborhood Churches 135
Courtyards and Hidden Gardens 139
Galleries and Museums of Art 143
Guggenheim Collection by Peggy 143
Gallery of the Academy 148
Museo Correr 152
Venetian Islands 156
Murano 156
Torcello: A Calm Retreat 160
CHAPTER 5 165
THE VENTIAN CULTURE 165
Etiquette and Customs in the Area 165
Traditions and Festivals in Venice 169
Language Advice for Travelers 174
CHAPTER 6 179
VENICE'S CUISINE AND DRINKS 179
Things to Try in Venetian Cuisine 179
Where to Get Food and Drink 182
Experiences with Food 186
CHAPTER 7 191
NAVIGATING VENICE 191
Strolling about Venice 191
Options for Public Transportation 195

Gondola Rides: A Timeless Adventure 199
CHAPTER 8 204
VENICE DAY TRIPS 204
   Exploring the Veneto Area 204
      Verona 204
      Padua 208
      Palladian Architecture in Vicenza 213
CHAPTER 9 219
USEFUL ADVICE FOR TRAVELERS 219
   How to Keep Safe in Venice 219
   Communication and Connectivity 223
   Venice's accessibility 227
CONCLUSION 232

INTRODUCTION

Venice is more than just a city; it's an experience, a location that seems to be from a different era. The city is located on water, with canals for streets, boats for automobiles, and a little of history hidden around every corner. Venice has captivated tourists, artists, and visionaries for centuries, and it still astounds millions of tourists each year. This book is intended to help you understand what makes Venice so unique while also providing you with all the information you need to fully appreciate the city.

Venice seems to have been created with admiration in mind. With its magnificent palaces, ancient cathedrals, and quaint bridges that appear to float on the river, its beauty is obvious. The canals and the vibrant houses that flank them make for an almost dreamlike scene. However, Venice is more than its appearance. The city has more than a thousand years of fascinating and rich history. Once a hub of trade and culture that linked Europe and the East, it was one of the most powerful cities on earth. Its art, architecture, and customs still reflect its riches and power today. You will experience a sense of time travel as you traverse its numerous bridges and wind through its winding streets.

You can easily navigate Venice with the help of this guide. It is full with helpful information, insider secrets, and helpful suggestions to make your vacation as easy and pleasurable as possible. This book has answers to all of your questions, including when to go, how to get around, where to stay, and what to eat. However, it goes beyond the fundamentals. Additionally, this book seeks to facilitate your understanding of Venice's culture, people, and way of life. Curiosity is rewarded in Venice, and this book will inspire you to venture beyond of the popular tourist destinations to find the undiscovered treasures that contribute to the city's distinctiveness.

Venice's distinction from other cities is among the first things you'll notice about it. Roads as we know them are gone, as are buses and cars. Rather, you'll discover canals, boats, and winding passageways that may be both lovely and perplexing. In Venice, getting lost is like a rite of passage, and it's frequently at these moments that you discover the most breathtaking and surprising locations. In addition to assisting you with navigation, this book will inspire you to enjoy the thrill of exploring Venice on your own without a plan. Sometimes letting Venice surprise you is the greatest way to experience it.

Venice is a contrast-rich city. It is timeless and ever-evolving, grand and private, bustling and serene. The prominent sights, such as the Rialto Bridge and St. Mark's Basilica, are magnificent and deserving of their notoriety. However, the calmer, less crowded areas of Venice are where some of the most unforgettable experiences may be found. It could be a quiet café where residents go for coffee, a secret garden with a lovely fountain, or a small plaza where kids are playing. The quieter, more intimate encounters that make Venice so unique may be balanced with the must-see landmarks, as this book will demonstrate.

Another significant aspect of the Venetian experience is the cuisine. The food of the city is straightforward but flavorful, emphasizing local, fresh ingredients. There is something for every taste and price range, from seafood meals like risotto al nero di seppia (squid ink risotto) to little appetizers called cicchetti. Venice is also well-known for its bacari, or wine bars, where you may savor a plate of delectable appetizers and a glass of the local wine. Whether you're searching for a posh restaurant with a view of the Grand Canal or a small, quiet spot in the city, this guide will help you find the greatest places to dine and drink.

Venice is a city rich in customs as well. Venice has a rich cultural legacy that is ingrained in its past, from its well-known Carnival, which features intricate masks and costumes, to its centuries-old glass and lace industries. This tutorial will provide you with an overview of these customs and demonstrate how to participate in them. There are numerous opportunities to engage with Venice's culture, such as going to a glassblowing class on the island of Murano, taking in the vibrant homes of Burano, or going to a local celebration.

However, Venice is not without its difficulties. The city has to deal with the demands of tourism, environmental problems, and contemporary life. It's crucial for tourists to travel sensibly and to be aware of these difficulties. This book will provide you advice on how to appreciate Venice's surroundings, people, and culture while having fun. You may contribute to keeping Venice a lively and friendly destination for future generations by making wise decisions.

There is more to this book than simply advising you on where to go and what to do. It aims to help you comprehend Venice and see it as a place with a distinct personality and soul rather than just a tourist attraction. Giving you the resources to design your own Venetian vacation based on your tastes and interests is the goal. Regardless of your interests—art, history, cuisine, or just taking in the splendor of this amazing city—this guide has plenty to offer.

There is a lot of information in this book that will help you plan your vacation, get around the city, and make the most of your stay in Venice. More than that, though, you'll find motivation—motivation to discover, to educate yourself, and to engage with a city that has won so many people over. Venice is a city that makes an impression on your spirit and remains with you long after you leave. I sincerely hope that this book will enable you to have a memorable and significant time in Venice.

Therefore, this book is here to help you realize your aspirations, whether they involve riding in a gondola around the canals, admiring the art and architecture of St. Mark's Square, or just relaxing in a café with an espresso and taking in the scenery. There is a lot to discover in Venice, which is waiting for you. As you set off on a journey that will take you to one of the most stunning and distinctive cities in the world, let this book serve as your guide. Greetings from Venice, where your adventure starts.

THE REASON WHY VENICE IS AN ESSENTIAL TRAVEL DESTINATION

It should come as no surprise that tourists from all over the world regard Venice to be one of the most distinctive and fascinating towns in the world. The fact that Venice is unlike any other place you will ever see is what makes it so unique. With canals for streets and boats as the main means of mobility, this city is located on water and lacks both roads and automobiles. This alone distinguishes Venice from other cities, but its unique design is just one aspect of it. Venice is an incredibly beautiful city with a rich history, a thriving culture, and enduring charm. It is a location that seems to be from a different time period, but it nevertheless prospers in the contemporary world. Experiencing a lifestyle that is entirely distinct from what most people are accustomed to is the main reason for traveling to Venice.

The stunning beauty of Venice is among the first things that tourists notice. The city is composed of more than 100 tiny islands that are connected by bridges and canals, resulting in a charming and scenic setting. Grand palaces, ancient churches, and vibrant structures that appear to emerge out of the ocean are all examples of the breathtaking architecture. The canals, which are dotted with little boats and gondolas, enhance the city's allure and give it a romantic feel that is difficult to find anywhere. Whether it's a busy area with plenty of people, a towering church with elaborate features, or a peaceful canal shaded by old buildings, every part of Venice seems to offer a picture-perfect view. Venice's charm lies not only in its well-known sites but also in the little, commonplace scenes that give the city a vibrant, enchanted sense.

In addition to its stunning appearance, Venice has an intriguing past. It was established more than 1,500 years ago, and during the Middle Ages and the Renaissance, it rose to prominence as one of the world's most prosperous and powerful towns. Venice was a significant hub for trade that linked Europe and the East, bringing products, concepts, and cultures together in ways that influenced the modern world. Over the ages, the city's art, architecture, and customs have all been preserved to reflect its heritage. Since many of Venice's streets and structures haven't altered in hundreds of years, it's like traveling back in time. You can see and feel the city's history as you stroll through its streets, visit its museums, and take in its landmarks; it's not just something you read about in books.

Often referred to as the city's center, St. Mark's Square is one of Venice's most recognizable locations. Some of Venice's most well-known sites, such as the Doge's Palace, the Campanile (bell tower), and St. Mark's Basilica, are located on this expansive plaza. St. Mark's Basilica, with its golden mosaics, elaborate embellishments, and magnificent domes, is a masterpiece of Byzantine architecture. Once the home of Venice's rulers, the Doge's Palace, with its opulent rooms, exquisite artwork, and intriguing past, is a representation of the city's richness and power. Visitors can experience Venice from a new angle thanks to the Campanile's expansive views of the city and the surrounding lagoon. Another bustling spot where people congregate to take in the sights, listen to music, and enjoy the ambiance is St. Mark's Square. It is a must-see location for anyone traveling to Venice since it perfectly encapsulates the city.

Venice's culture is another factor that makes it an essential travel destination. Venice has a rich history of craftsmanship, music, and art that is still very much alive today. Some of the finest musicians and artists in history, such as Vivaldi, Tintoretto, and Titian, were born in the city. Its cathedrals and palaces are embellished with magnificent frescoes, sculptures, and paintings, and its museums and galleries are brimming with works of art that highlight the city's cultural legacy. Venice is also well-known for its customs and celebrations, which give the city a distinctive and fascinating feel. One of the most well-known celebrations worldwide, the Carnival of Venice draws tourists from all over the world with its extravagant masks and costumes. A more true and local taste of Venice's culture can be had during other events like the Festa del Redentore, a religious celebration with fireworks, and the Regata Storica, a historic boat race.

Another significant aspect of the Venetian experience is the cuisine. With a focus on using local, fresh products, the city's food is straightforward but tasty. Because Venice is surrounded by water and has access to some of the freshest fish and shellfish, seafood is a major component of Venetian cuisine. Venice offers a variety of unusual flavors, such as baccalà mantecato (creamed cod), sarde in saor (sweet and sour sardines), and risotto al nero di seppia (squid ink risotto).

The city is also well-known for its cicchetti, which are little appetizers that are frequently offered in neighborhood pubs called bacari with a glass of wine. Eating in Venice is more than simply the cuisine; it's also about taking in the atmosphere of this amazing city while dining by a canal.

Another city of contrasts is Venice. It is timeless and ever-evolving, opulent and private, busy and serene. There are peaceful areas of the city where you may get away from the crowds and see a more genuine side of Venice, even if the major tourist destinations, such as St. Mark's Basilica and the Rialto Bridge, are constantly packed with visitors. You might come onto a tiny area where kids are playing, a peaceful canal with a lone gondola, or a modest café where locals congregate for coffee while meandering through the winding alleyways and secret passageways. What makes Venice so unique and memorable are these epiphanies.

Venice's distinctiveness is another factor that makes it an essential travel destination. It is the only location of its kind in the entire world. With its canals and bridges, the city's design evokes an indescribable sense of wonder and adventure. Navigating Venice is an adventure in and of itself, whether you choose to ride a gondola through the smaller canals, take a vaporetto (water bus) down the Grand Canal, or stroll through its winding streets. A tranquil and soothing ambiance is created by the lack of automobiles and the sound of the water rather than traffic, which is uncommon in the hectic world of today. You may slow down, appreciate the beauty all around you, and savor the present in Venice.

Venice is a city that makes an impact. It is a city that captivates you and makes you want to go back, a place that remains with you long after you have left. Venice has a way of giving every visitor the impression that they have witnessed something genuinely unique, whether it be the splendor of its canals, the depth of its history, the friendliness of its people, or the enchantment of its ambiance. It is a city that serves as a reminder of both the value of embracing the present while preserving the past and the creative potential of people. Venice is a must-see location that ought to be on everyone's travel itinerary for all of these reasons and more.

VENICE'S HISTORY

One of the most intriguing tales in the world is the history of Venice. It tells the tale of a city that was founded on water, grew to become one of the most prosperous and powerful towns in history, and overcame innumerable obstacles to endure for more than a millennium. Venice is more than just a city; it is a representation of the inventiveness, tenacity, and inventiveness of people. It is crucial to examine Venice's past in order to comprehend how it became what it is now.

Venice's beginnings date back to the fifth century AD, when Europe was experiencing a tremendous deal of unrest. Barbarian incursions were spreading throughout the continent, and the Roman Empire was in decline. In order to avoid the violence and devastation, residents of northern Italy, especially in cities like Padua, Treviso, and Aquileia, were compelled to leave their homes. A large number of them took sanctuary on the marshy islands of the Adriatic Sea's Venetian Lagoon, a shallow body of water. These islands provided a safe haven for persons in need of refuge since they were challenging to reach and provided defense against invaders. Initially, the residents of the lagoon maintained modest lives, making their living from trade, salt manufacture, and fishing. They used boats to travel between the islands and raised their houses on wooden stilts to keep them above the sea.

The lagoon's little settlements started to develop and band together over time. They had established a loose federation of communities by the 7th century, and in 697 AD they chose the

Doge as their first ruler. The Doge served as the head of state and was heavily involved in city governance. This signaled the start of the Venetian Republic, a novel system of governance that would endure for more than a millennium. Venice was not governed by a monarch or aristocratic family, in contrast to many other European towns. Rather, it was run by a system of elected councils and officials, which provided it with a level of stability and independence uncommon at the time.

Venice's growth was significantly influenced by its location in the lagoon. The city was a perfect hub for trade because it was located at the intersection of major trade routes between Europe and the East. Venice had become a significant commerce hub by the ninth century, and its merchants were buying and selling products all the way to the Islamic world and the Byzantine Empire. The city gained notoriety for its affluence and wealth, and its power started to increase. St. Mark the Evangelist became the patron saint of Venice in 828 AD after Venetian traders transported his remains from Alexandria to the city. Soon after, work on St. Mark's Basilica, one of Venice's most recognizable monuments, started, signifying the city's increasing strength and renown.

Venice kept growing in wealth and power during the Middle Ages. With a fleet of ships that dominated trade in the Mediterranean and beyond, it rose to prominence as a maritime power. Trade was the backbone of the city's economy, and its merchants traded in a variety of commodities, such as precious metals, silk, and spices. Venice also developed into a major shipbuilding hub, manufacturing some of the most cutting-edge vessels of the era at its renowned Arsenal. The city established colonies and trading posts around the Mediterranean, notably in locations like Crete, Cyprus, and the Dalmatian coast, thanks to its advantageous location and potent navy. Venice's wealth and influence were further enhanced by these holdings, which also served to secure her trading routes.

The Renaissance, a time of economic and cultural prosperity that started in the 14th century, was when Venice's influence peaked. Venice rose to prominence as one of Europe's most significant cities, renowned for its intellectual accomplishments, art, and architecture. Some of the greatest artists and architects of the era, such as Titian, Tintoretto, and Palladio, were born in the city; their creations are still on display in Venice today. With its printing presses creating some of the first books in Europe, the Venetian Republic also made significant contributions to the development of printing. Venice became a symbol of the Renaissance and a lighthouse of civilization due to its wealth and cultural accomplishments.

But Venice's prosperity also presented difficulties. Other maritime nations who aimed to dominate Mediterranean trade, including Genoa and the Ottoman Empire, competed with the city. Venice's economic significance decreased in the 15th century as a result of the discovery of new trade routes to the Americas and Asia, which diverted attention from the Mediterranean to other regions of the world. Social instability and governmental corruption were among the city's internal problems. Venice was able to preserve its autonomy and remained a significant hub for the arts and culture in spite of these challenges.

As the city's economy and political influence waned in the 17th and 18th centuries, the Venetian Republic started to fall apart. Napoleon Bonaparte took control of Venice in 1797, and it joined the Austrian Empire. The Venetian Republic, which had existed for more than a millennium, came to an end with this. Venice lost a lot of its autonomy and power under Austrian control, but it continued to be a significant hub for the arts and culture. Venice joined the newly unified Kingdom of Italy in 1866 and has remained a part of Italy ever since.

Venice has maintained its distinct identity and character in spite of the difficulties it has encountered. The city's art, architecture, and customs all exhibit remnants of its past that have been meticulously conserved over the ages. Today, Venice is one of the world's most visited tourist attractions and a UNESCO World Heritage Site. You can see and feel its history as you stroll through its streets, cross its bridges, and explore its canals; it is not merely something that is written in books. The tale of Venice, a city on water that became one of the greatest cities in history, is a tribute to the tenacity and inventiveness of its citizens.

CHAPTER 1

ORGANIZING YOUR VACATION TO VENICE

When to Go to Venice

What you hope to get out of your trip will determine the ideal time to visit Venice. Every season offers a unique experience in Venice, a city that transforms with the seasons. Your trip will be influenced by a number of factors, including the weather, the volume of visitors, and the events taking place in the city. Making the most of your time in this exceptional and stunning city can be achieved by knowing the seasons and what they bring. Although you can visit Venice at any time of year, the experience will change based on whether you go in the spring, summer, fall, or winter. Every season has its own unique appeal, and being aware of what to anticipate will make your vacation planning easier.

One of the most well-liked seasons to visit Venice is spring, which spans from March to May. Temperatures during this season range from about 10°C (50°F) in March to 20°C (68°F) or higher in May, with generally mild and pleasant weather. After the chilly winter months, the city comes alive as the days become longer. Venice is best explored on foot in the spring when the weather is pleasant and the architecture and canals are particularly lovely in the warm spring sunlight. Although the number of tourists does begin to rise as the season goes on, the city is not as busy as it is during the summer. The Feast of the Ascension, also known as the Festa della Sensa, is held in May and is one of the highlights of Venice's spring season. The mayor of Venice tosses a ring into the water to "marry" the sea in a symbolic ceremony that honors Venice's longstanding relationship with the sea. Additionally, the celebration includes a boat race, or regatta, which is a great way to witness the city's maritime customs in action.

The busiest travel season in Venice is summer, which runs from June to August. Due to the large number of tourists from across the globe, the city's major attractions, like the Rialto Bridge and St. Mark's Basilica, can get quite crowded. Summertime temperatures are warm, frequently rising to 30°C (86°F) or more in July and August. Particularly in the afternoons, the city can feel quite hot and muggy due to the heat and the humidity from the lagoon. But summer is also a period when Venice comes alive with activity and vitality.

Gondola rides, walks along the canals, and outdoor dining are all made possible by the long days and warm evenings. The July Feast of the Redeemer, also known as the Festa del Redentore, is one of the most well-known summertime festivals in Venice. One of the most unforgettable sights you may see in Venice is the stunning fireworks show that takes place over the lagoon during this religious holiday. The Venice Film Festival, which takes place on the nearby island of Lido in late August or early September, is another important summer event. Celebrities and movie buffs from all over the world come to this esteemed festival, which gives the city a glamorous touch.

Many people believe that the greatest time to visit Venice is in the fall, or autumn, which runs from September to November. With temperatures ranging from about 20°C (68°F) in September to 10°C (50°F) or lower in November, the weather is more comfortable and colder than it is in the summer. Summertime crowds start to disperse, particularly in October and November, which makes it simpler to take in the city's highlights without feeling overcrowded. Fall in Venice is a particularly lovely time of year for light, with golden sunsets reflecting off the lake and creating a mystical ambiance. As fresh seafood, truffles, and other regional specialties are in season, fall is also a fantastic time to explore Venice's culinary and wine traditions. The September Regata Storica, often known as the Historical Regatta, is one of the most important autumnal festivities in Venice. Following a vibrant parade of historic boats, there will be a number of Grand Canal rowing competitions. It is a fantastic chance to witness the history and customs of Venice come to life. The Biennale, an international art exhibition that happens every two years and frequently lasts into the fall, is another occasion to think about. Art enthusiasts should not miss the Biennale, which features modern artwork from all over the world.

The slowest travel season in Venice is winter, which runs from December to February. You can have a more tranquil and private experience because the city is far less congested than it is in the spring or summer. Wintertime temperatures range from about 0°C (32°F) to 10°C (50°F), and the lagoon frequently creates a damp chill in the air. However, winter is a unique time to visit Venice because of the absence of visitors and the city's distinct vibe. With mist rising from the canals and footfall reverberating through the winding alleyways, the city assumes a magical and enigmatic air. Acqua alta, or high water, which happens as the tide rises and floods areas of the city, is also more likely to occur during the winter. Even while it can be annoying, this is an intriguing occurrence that contributes to Venice's unique character. The Carnival, held in February, is one of the most spectacular events of Venice's winter season. One of the most well-known celebrations worldwide, the Carnival of Venice is renowned for its ornate parades, masks, and costumes. A memorable time to visit, the city comes alive with dancing, music, and festivities. Christmas is another wintertime event to think of, when Venice is decked out in spectacular displays and lights, making it feel cozy and inviting.

Examples of Itineraries

Sample Itineraries for Three Days

The ideal length of time to see the main attractions of this distinctive city while still finding time to take in its ambiance and charm is three days. Venice's small size makes it perfect for exploring on foot or by boat, and every nook feels like a piece of art. You have three days to see the city's most well-known sites, take in its fascinating history and culture, and even visit some of the neighboring islands in the lagoon.

Making the most of your time in Venice is the goal of this itinerary, which strikes a balance between sightseeing and leisure time to take in the city's renowned slower pace of life. Every day is meticulously organized to make sure you see the most of Venice without feeling hurried and to allow for the most memorable parts of any trip—the unanticipated discoveries.

St. Mark's Square, also known as Piazza San Marco, is the ideal place to start your first day in Venice. Some of Venice's most significant landmarks may be found in this area, which is also its most well-known and iconic. Start your day early to beat the crowds and enjoy the square's splendor, which is encircled by old buildings and occasionally inhabited by pigeons and church bells. St. Mark's Basilica, a magnificent church and a masterwork of Byzantine architecture, ought certainly be the first destination. It is among the most magnificent attractions in Venice because of its golden mosaics, elaborate embellishments, and striking domes. Make sure to visit the museum on the higher floor, which has a balcony overlooking the square, and go inside to see the mosaics up close. Proceed to the Doge's Palace, which is directly next door, after touring the basilica. The Doge, the ruler of Venice, once lived in this magnificent structure, which represents the richness and power of the city at its prime. You can explore the lavish corridors, take in the artwork, and traverse the well-known Bridge of Sighs, which links the palace and the former jail. Spend some time admiring the square itself after seeing these two landmarks. Enjoy a coffee or a small snack while taking in the scenery at one of the outdoor cafés, like the iconic Caffè Florian. Enjoy stunning views of the lagoon and the neighboring islands while strolling along the Riva degli Schiavoni waterfront promenade in the afternoon. To see the city from a new angle, you may also take a quick ride in a gondola or a vaporetto (water bus) along the Grand Canal. Savor regional specialties like sarde in saor (sweet and sour sardines) or risotto al nero di seppia (squid ink risotto) over a relaxed meal at a traditional Venetian restaurant to cap off your first day.

Spend your second day in Venice discovering the city's hidden treasures and neighborhoods. The renowned Rialto Bridge and the lively Rialto Market can be found in the Rialto neighborhood, where you should begin your day. One of Venice's most recognizable landmarks, the bridge provides breathtaking views of the Grand Canal. Spend some time strolling across the bridge and perusing the stores that line it, offering everything from souvenirs to jewelry. Locals visit the nearby Rialto Market to purchase fresh produce, seafood, and other items. One of the best ways to view the range of ingredients used in the city's cuisine and to get a taste of Venetian daily life is to visit the market. Visit the Cannaregio neighborhood, one of Venice's most sedate and genuine areas, after touring the Rialto region. This area is well-known for its quaint canals, old buildings, and laid-back vibe. The Jewish Ghetto, one of the oldest and most historically significant in Europe, is also located there. You can stroll through the charming streets and take in the serene surroundings, or you can visit the Jewish Museum and the ancient synagogues. Travel to the Dorsoduro district in the afternoon; this area is renowned for its culture and art. The Peggy Guggenheim Collection is a museum of modern art located in a stunning palazzo along the Grand Canal. The museum is a must-see for art enthusiasts and exhibits pieces by painters like Picasso, Pollock, and Dalí. Following your visit to the museum, stroll down the Zattere promenade, which is an excellent spot to watch the sunset and gives breathtaking views of the Giudecca Canal. Visit a neighborhood bacaro, or wine bar, to cap off your second day. There, you can sip wine and cicchetti, or tiny nibbles, in a welcoming and informal atmosphere.

Enjoy the chance to tour the islands of the Venetian Lagoon on your third and last day in Venice. Visit Murano, which is well-known for its glassmaking heritage, to start your day. To witness how the elaborate glass items are created, you can ride a vaporetto to the island and stop by one of the many glass factories and workshops. The Glass Museum, which displays the art and history of glassmaking in Venice, is also located in Murano. Visit the neighboring island of Burano, which is well-known for its vibrant homes and lace-making customs, after touring Murano. The island's colorful buildings make for a picturesque scene, and it's a terrific spot for leisurely strolls and photo ops. To learn more about this age-old craft, you can also stop by the Lace Museum or one of the lace stores. Consider spending some time on the island of Torcello, which has a more tranquil and rustic feel and is home to some of the lagoon's oldest towns. Torcello is the location of the Devil's Bridge, a little but significant stone bridge, and the Cathedral of Santa Maria Assunta, which has exquisite mosaics. Return to Venice in the late afternoon after touring the islands, and spend your last evening taking in the ambience of the city. You can stroll down the Grand Canal, stop by a neighborhood store to buy trinkets, or just relax by the water and think back on your stay in this amazing city. Consider having your final meal in Venice in a restaurant overlooking the canal or lagoon, where you can savor a delectable meal while taking in the city's lights as they reflect on the water.

This three-day tour covers Venice's most well-known sites, as well as its lesser-known spots and neighboring islands, to offer you a well-rounded experience. It gives you time to unwind and take in the city's own character while also letting you view its main attractions. There is always something new to find in Venice, a city that inspires exploration regardless of how much time you spend there. You can get the most out of your trip and produce lifelong memories by sticking to this schedule.

Sample Itineraries for Five Days

The ideal time to completely see the beauty, history, and culture of this remarkable city is during a five-day journey to Venice. You have five days to see Venice's most well-known sites, stroll around its more sedate areas, take in its distinctive customs, and even visit the nearby islands in the lagoon. Making the most of your time in Venice is the goal of this schedule, which strikes a balance between sightseeing and downtime to take in the ambience of the city. With five days, you may delve deeper and really experience Venice's beauty and personality. The city rewards leisurely exploration. Every day is thoughtfully organized to make sure you see the most of

Venice without feeling hurried and to allow for unforeseen discoveries, which are frequently the highlights of any trip.

St. Mark's Square, also known as Piazza San Marco, is the ideal place to start your first day in Venice. Some of Venice's most significant landmarks may be found in this area, which is also its most well-known and iconic. Start your day early to beat the crowds and enjoy the square's splendor, which is encircled by old buildings and occasionally inhabited by pigeons and church bells. St. Mark's Basilica, a magnificent church and a masterwork of Byzantine architecture, ought certainly be the first destination. It is among the most magnificent attractions in Venice because of its golden mosaics, elaborate embellishments, and striking domes. Make sure to visit the museum on the higher floor, which has a balcony overlooking the square, and go inside to see the mosaics up close. Proceed to the Doge's Palace, which is directly next door, after touring the basilica. The Doge, the ruler of Venice, once lived in this magnificent structure, which represents the richness and power of the city at its prime. You can explore the lavish corridors, take in the artwork, and traverse the well-known Bridge of Sighs, which links the palace and the former jail. Spend some time admiring the square itself after seeing these two landmarks. Enjoy a coffee or a small snack while taking in the scenery at one of the outdoor cafés, like the iconic Caffè Florian. Enjoy stunning views of the lagoon and the neighboring islands while strolling along the Riva degli Schiavoni waterfront promenade in the afternoon. To see the city from a new angle, you may also take a quick ride in a gondola or a vaporetto (water bus) along the

Grand Canal. Savor regional specialties like sarde in saor (sweet and sour sardines) or risotto al nero di seppia (squid ink risotto) over a relaxed meal at a traditional Venetian restaurant to cap off your first day.

Spend your second day in Venice discovering the city's hidden treasures and neighborhoods. The renowned Rialto Bridge and the lively Rialto Market can be found in the Rialto neighborhood, where you should begin your day. One of Venice's most recognizable landmarks, the bridge provides breathtaking views of the Grand Canal. Spend some time strolling across the bridge and perusing the stores that line it, offering everything from souvenirs to jewelry. Locals visit the nearby Rialto Market to purchase fresh produce, seafood, and other items. One of the best ways to view the range of ingredients used in the city's cuisine and to get a taste of Venetian daily life is to visit the market. Visit the Cannaregio neighborhood, one of Venice's most sedate and genuine areas, after touring the Rialto region. This area is well-known for its quaint canals, old buildings, and laid-back vibe. The Jewish Ghetto, one of the oldest and most historically significant in Europe, is also located there. You can stroll through the charming streets and take in the serene surroundings, or you can visit the Jewish Museum and the ancient synagogues.

Travel to the Dorsoduro district in the afternoon; this area is renowned for its culture and art. The Peggy Guggenheim Collection is a museum of modern art located in a stunning palazzo along the Grand Canal. The museum is a must-see for art enthusiasts and exhibits pieces by painters like Picasso,

Pollock, and Dalí. Following your visit to the museum, stroll down the Zattere promenade, which is an excellent spot to watch the sunset and gives breathtaking views of the Giudecca Canal. Visit a neighborhood bacaro, or wine bar, to cap off your second day. There, you can sip wine and cicchetti, or tiny nibbles, in a welcoming and informal atmosphere.

Enjoy the chance to tour the Venetian Lagoon's islands on your third day there. Visit Murano, which is well-known for its glassmaking heritage, to start your day. To witness how the elaborate glass items are created, you can ride a vaporetto to the island and stop by one of the many glass factories and workshops. The Glass Museum, which displays the art and history of glassmaking in Venice, is also located in Murano. Visit the neighboring island of Burano, which is well-known for its vibrant homes and lace-making customs, after touring Murano. The island's colorful buildings make for a picturesque scene, and it's a terrific spot for leisurely strolls and photo ops.

To learn more about this age-old craft, you can also stop by the Lace Museum or one of the lace stores. Consider spending some time on the island of Torcello, which has a more tranquil and rustic feel and is home to some of the lagoon's oldest towns. Torcello is the location of the Devil's Bridge, a little but significant stone bridge, and the Cathedral of Santa Maria Assunta, which has exquisite mosaics. Return to Venice in the late afternoon after touring the islands, and then spend the evening taking in the ambience of the city. You can stroll down the Grand Canal, stop by a neighborhood store to buy trinkets, or just relax by the water and think back on your stay in this amazing city.

Spend some time exploring Venice's lesser-known sights and taking in its distinct vibe on your fourth day there. Visit the Basilica di Santa Maria della Salute, a stunning basilica at the Grand Canal's entry, first thing in the morning. One of Venice's most recognizable structures, this church was constructed in the 17th century as a thank-you gift to the Virgin Mary for sparing the city from a plague. Following your visit to the basilica, stroll around the neighboring Punta della Dogana, a museum of modern art set in a former customs house. The museum offers breathtaking views of St. Mark's Basin and the Grand Canal, as well as changing exhibitions of modern art. Visit one of Venice's biggest and most varied areas, the Castello district, in the afternoon. The Arsenale, a historic shipyard that was important to Venice's maritime history, is located in this region. The Venice Biennale, an international art show that happens every two years, is held at the Biennale Gardens, which you may also visit. The gardens offer a tranquil spot to unwind and take in the scenery. Visit a classic Venetian trattoria to cap off your fourth day, where you can savor a substantial dinner of pasta, shellfish, or other regional favorites.

Enjoy the chance to explore any sites you may have missed or return to your favorite spots on your fifth and last day in Venice. After enjoying a leisurely breakfast at a neighborhood café, you can take a stroll around the city's squares and streets to start your day. Consider taking a gondola ride around the smaller canals if you haven't already; it provides a more private and romantic perspective of the city. You may also explore some of Venice's smaller galleries and museums, including the Scuola Grande di San Rocco, which has beautiful pieces by Tintoretto, or the Ca' Rezzonico, a museum of Venetian art and culture from the 18th century. Spend some time in the afternoon shopping for delightful mementos of your journey, including Venetian masks, Burano lace, or Murano glass. You can get one last look at the city's splendor by taking a sunset boat on the lagoon or a final stroll along the Grand Canal. Select a restaurant with a view of the water for your last meal so you can have a delectable meal while taking in the reflection of Venice's lights on the canals.

This five-day itinerary covers Venice's most well-known sites, as well as its lesser-known spots and neighboring islands, to provide you with a thorough and unforgettable trip. It gives you time to unwind and take in the city's own character while also letting you view its main attractions. There is always something new to find in Venice, a city that inspires exploration regardless of how much time you spend there. You can get the most out of your trip and produce lifelong memories by sticking to this schedule.

Sample Itineraries for Seven Days

To really see Venice's beauty, history, and culture, a seven-day journey is the perfect length of time. You may take your time seeing Venice for a full week, seeing not just its most well-known sites but also its more obscure areas, more sedate neighborhoods, and the neighboring islands of the lagoon. Spending seven days in Venice allows you to experience its distinct ambiance, admire its art and architecture, and savor its culinary customs. Venice is a city that welcomes leisurely investigation. By striking a balance between sightseeing and leisure time, this plan is intended to help you get the most out of your trip to Venice. Every day is thoughtfully organized to make sure you see the most of Venice without feeling hurried and to allow for unforeseen discoveries, which are frequently the highlights of any trip.

St. Mark's Square, also known as Piazza San Marco, is the ideal place to start your first day in Venice. Some of Venice's most significant landmarks may be found in this area, which is also its most well-known and iconic. Start your day early to beat the crowds and enjoy the square's splendor, which is encircled by old buildings and occasionally inhabited by pigeons and church bells. St. Mark's Basilica, a magnificent church and a masterwork of Byzantine architecture, ought certainly be the first destination. It is among the most magnificent attractions in Venice because of its golden mosaics, elaborate embellishments, and striking domes. Make sure to visit the museum on the higher floor, which has a balcony overlooking the square, and go inside to see the mosaics up close. Proceed to the Doge's Palace, which is directly next door, after touring the basilica. The Doge, the ruler of Venice, once lived in this magnificent structure, which represents the richness and power of the city at its prime. You can explore the lavish corridors, take in the artwork, and traverse the well-known Bridge of Sighs, which links the palace and the former jail. Spend some time admiring the square itself after seeing these two landmarks. Enjoy a coffee or a small snack while taking in the scenery at one of the outdoor cafés, like the iconic Caffè Florian. Enjoy stunning views of the lagoon and the neighboring islands while strolling along the Riva degli Schiavoni waterfront promenade in the afternoon. To see the city from a new angle, you may also take a quick ride in a gondola or a vaporetto (water bus) along the Grand Canal. Savor regional specialties like sarde in saor (sweet and sour sardines) or risotto al nero di seppia (squid ink risotto) over a relaxed meal at a traditional Venetian restaurant to cap off your first day.

Spend your second day in Venice discovering the city's hidden treasures and neighborhoods. The renowned Rialto Bridge and the lively Rialto Market can be found in the Rialto neighborhood, where you should begin your day. One of Venice's most recognizable landmarks, the bridge provides breathtaking views of the Grand Canal. Spend some time strolling across the bridge and perusing the stores that line it, offering everything from souvenirs to jewelry. Locals visit the nearby Rialto Market to purchase fresh produce, seafood, and other items. One of the best ways to view the range of ingredients used in the city's cuisine and to get a taste of Venetian daily life is to visit the market. Visit the Cannaregio neighborhood, one of Venice's most sedate and genuine areas, after touring the Rialto region. This area is well-known for its quaint canals, old buildings, and laid-back vibe. The Jewish Ghetto, one of the oldest and most historically significant in Europe, is also located there. You can stroll through the charming streets and take in the serene surroundings, or you can visit the Jewish Museum and the ancient synagogues. Travel to the Dorsoduro district in the afternoon; this area is renowned for its culture and art. The Peggy Guggenheim Collection is a museum of modern art located in a stunning palazzo along the Grand Canal. The museum is a must-see for art enthusiasts and exhibits pieces by painters like Picasso, Pollock, and Dalí. Following your visit to the museum, stroll down the Zattere promenade, which is an excellent spot to watch the sunset and gives breathtaking views of the Giudecca Canal. Visit a neighborhood bacaro, or wine bar, to cap off your second day. There, you can sip wine and cicchetti, or tiny nibbles, in a welcoming and informal atmosphere.

Enjoy the chance to tour the Venetian Lagoon's islands on your third day there. Visit Murano, which is well-known for its glassmaking heritage, to start your day. To witness how the elaborate glass items are created, you can ride a vaporetto to the island and stop by one of the many glass factories and workshops. The Glass Museum, which displays the art and history of glassmaking in Venice, is also located in Murano. Visit the neighboring island of Burano, which is well-known for its vibrant homes and lace-making customs, after touring Murano. The island's colorful buildings make for a picturesque scene, and it's a terrific spot for leisurely strolls and photo ops. To learn more about this age-old craft, you can also stop by the Lace Museum or one of the lace stores. Consider spending some time on the island of Torcello, which has a more tranquil and rustic feel and is home to some of the lagoon's oldest towns. Torcello is the location of the Devil's Bridge, a little but significant stone bridge, and the Cathedral of Santa Maria Assunta, which has exquisite mosaics. Return to Venice in the late afternoon after touring the islands, and then spend the evening taking in the ambience of the city. You can stroll down the Grand Canal, stop by a neighborhood store to buy trinkets, or just relax by the water and think back on your stay in this amazing city.

Spend some time exploring Venice's lesser-known sights and taking in its distinct vibe on your fourth day there. Visit the Basilica di Santa Maria della Salute, a stunning basilica at the Grand Canal's entry, first thing in the morning. One of Venice's most recognizable structures, this church was constructed in the 17th century as a thank-you gift to the Virgin Mary for sparing the city from a plague. Following your visit to the basilica, stroll around the neighboring Punta della Dogana, a museum of modern art set in a former customs house. The museum offers breathtaking views of St. Mark's Basin and the Grand Canal, as well as changing exhibitions of modern art. Visit one of Venice's biggest and most varied areas, the Castello district, in the afternoon. The Arsenale, a historic shipyard that was important to Venice's maritime history, is located in this region. The Venice Biennale, an international art show that happens every two years, is held at the Biennale Gardens, which you may also visit. The gardens offer a tranquil spot to unwind and take in the scenery. Visit a classic Venetian trattoria to cap off your fourth day, where you can savor a substantial dinner of pasta, shellfish, or other regional favorites.

Think about going on a day trip to one of the neighboring cities or towns that are conveniently accessible from Venice on your fifth day. Verona, for instance, is a picturesque city well-known for its Roman amphitheater and its association with Romeo and Juliet by Shakespeare. A train ride to Padua, a medieval city with lovely cathedrals, gardens, and a vibrant atmosphere, offers an alternative. Another choice is to travel to the Prosecco wine area, where you can taste some of Italy's best sparkling wines and tour vineyards. You may see more of the Veneto region and discover a new aspect of Italian culture with these day trips.

Return to Venice on your sixth day and spend the day exploring new regions or going back to your favorite spots. You can visit some of the city's smaller galleries and museums, take a gondola ride over one of the smaller canals, or just stroll around the squares and streets and take in the atmosphere. Consider going to a show at one of Venice's historic theaters in the evening, including La Fenice, which is well-known for its opera and classical music productions.

Spend some time relaxing and taking it leisurely on your seventh and last day in Venice. After enjoying a leisurely breakfast at a neighborhood café, you can visit a peaceful square or take a stroll along the Grand Canal. Shop for souvenirs during the day. Items like Venetian masks, Burano lace, and Murano glass are excellent mementos of your vacation. A last stroll along the waterfront or a sunset boat on the lagoon are great ways to round off your trip to Venice and enjoy the city's beauty one last time. Select a restaurant with a view of the water for your last meal so you can have a delectable meal while taking in the reflection of Venice's lights on the canals.

This seven-day itinerary covers Venice's most well-known sites, as well as its lesser-known spots and neighboring islands, to provide you with a thorough and unforgettable trip. It gives you time to unwind and take in the city's own character while also letting you view its main attractions. There is always something new to find in Venice, a city that inspires exploration regardless of how much time you spend there. You can get the most out of your trip and produce lifelong memories by sticking to this schedule.

Setting a Travel Budget

One of the most important aspects of organizing your vacation to Venice is creating a budget. Despite being one of the most costly travel destinations in Europe, Venice is renowned for its allure, history, and culture. On the other hand, you may enjoy Venice on a budget that works for you if you plan ahead and know exactly how much it will cost. Knowing the various costs you may face in Venice will help you make wise choices and steer clear of unpleasant surprises, regardless of whether you are a luxury traveler or someone trying to cut costs. Every element of your trip, from lodging and transportation to meals, sights, and other ancillary expenses, can be organized ahead of time to guarantee you have a great time without going over budget.

Accommodations are one of the biggest costs associated with any trip to Venice. From opulent hotels with views of the Grand Canal to affordable hostels and guesthouses, the city has a lot to offer. The time of year, the area, and the kind of hotel you select can all have a significant impact on the price of staying in Venice. Although convenient, lodging in Venice's historic center—especially close to St. Mark's Square or the Rialto Bridge—tends to be more costly. Staying in neighborhoods like Cannaregio or Dorsoduro, which are a little less central but still close to the main attractions, is a good option if you want to cut costs. Another option is to take a daily short rail or bus ride into Venice from Mestre, which is on the mainland and has hotels that are usually less expensive. To be sure you are receiving a decent deal, it is crucial to read reviews and compare costs before making a reservation. Lower prices can also be obtained by making reservations far in advance, particularly if you are visiting during the busiest travel times.

When planning your trip to Venice, transportation is yet another crucial component to take into account. The city is distinct in that all forms of mobility are done on foot or by boat, and there are neither vehicles nor roads. The vaporetto, or water bus, is the primary mode of public transportation in Venice. It travels through the canals and links the various areas of the city and the nearby islands. Since a single vaporetto ticket can be somewhat pricey, it is frequently more economical to buy a travel pass that grants unlimited rides for a predetermined amount of time, like 24, 48, or 72 hours. A weekly pass can be a wise choice if you intend to spend a number of days in Venice. Although gondola rides are among the most famous things to do in Venice, they are also very costly; a typical ride lasts between 80 and 100 euros for 30 minutes. Take a traghetto, a shared gondola that transports people across the Grand Canal for a far reduced cost, if you are on a tight budget but still want to enjoy a gondola. Because Venice is relatively small and the majority of the major sites are within walking distance of one another, strolling is also a fantastic way to travel around the city. Walking is not only free, but it also lets you take your time discovering Venice's winding alleyways and secret spots.

A trip to Venice would not be complete without food and drink, which, if you are not careful, may be very expensive. Venice offers a variety of dining options, including casual trattorias, street food vendors, and upscale restaurants. Avoid dining at establishments close to popular tourist destinations if you want to save money because they are typically more costly and serve tourists rather than locals. To experience real Venetian cuisine at a more affordable price, seek for smaller, family-run restaurants in less congested neighborhoods.

Eating like a local in a bacaro, a classic Venetian wine bar that sells little appetizers called cicchetti, is another method to cut costs on food. These are inexpensive ways to try a range of foods and are comparable to tapas. A popular and reasonably priced breakfast option in Italy is to stop by a café for a coffee and a croissant. You can also save money by shopping at local markets and food stores and cooking some of your own meals if you are staying in a place with a kitchen. Bring a reusable water bottle and fill it up at the public fountains, which give safe and clean drinking water, as purchasing bottled water all the time may get costly in Venice.

You'll also need to carefully consider your budget for activities and attractions. The Doge's Palace and St. Mark's Basilica, two of Venice's most well-known sites, require an admission price. Consider buying a city pass or combo ticket, which offers cheap admission to several attractions, to save money. For instance, the Chorus Pass grants admittance to various stunning churches in the city, while the Venice Museum Pass grants access to numerous museums and historic monuments. The Rialto Bridge and the squares and streets of Venice are two examples of sites that are free to enter and enjoy. Consider going to the Peggy Guggenheim Collection or the Gallerie dell'Accademia if you're interested in art; both places provide elders and students with cheap admission. Taking advantage of free events and experiences, like festivals or walking tours, which are frequently held all year long, is another method to cut costs on activities.

Your budget should also account for other costs like tips, travel insurance, and souvenirs. Venice is renowned for its distinctive crafts, which include Burano lace, Murano glass, and Venetian masks. These items can be highly costly but make excellent mementos. Establish a spending limit for mementos and research prices before making a purchase to prevent going overboard. Tipping is appreciated for excellent service, particularly in restaurants and for tour guides, although it is not required in Italy. Usually, a modest tip of five to ten percent is adequate. Another significant cost to take into account is travel insurance, which can cover unforeseen circumstances like medical crises, trip cancellations, or misplaced luggage. Travel insurance can save you money and give you peace of mind in the event that something goes wrong while you're traveling, even if it could seem like an extra expense.

Finally, it's critical to budget for unforeseen costs and allow for some leeway. Venice is full of surprises, so you might find chances for unusual activities that you hadn't planned for beforehand, like a private tour, a culinary class, or a special performance. Your trip will be much more memorable if you have a little extra cash saved up for these impromptu events. You may have a fantastic trip to Venice without worrying about going over budget if you carefully weigh all of these aspects and plan your spending beforehand. Venice has something to offer everyone, regardless of your travel budget or desire to indulge in a once-in-a-lifetime experience. With the correct planning, you can get the most out of your trip to this amazing city.

Essentials for your Trip

Things to Bring to Venice

To make sure you have everything you need for a relaxing and pleasurable journey, packing for a trip to Venice involves considerable consideration and preparation. Because Venice is a special city with its own set of difficulties and features, it's critical to bring products that are useful, adaptable, and appropriate for the surroundings. Every item on your packing list, from clothes and shoes to personal belongings and travel necessities, should be taken into account to prevent needless costs and problems while traveling. Making a packing budget is also a crucial step in the process because it enables you to pick the most critical goods and prevents you from splurging on products you might not need. You may save money, lessen stress, and make sure you are ready for your trip to Venice by taking the time to organize your packing list in advance.

The kind of clothing you will require is among the most crucial factors to take into account when packing for Venice. Depending on the season, Venice's weather can change significantly, so it's important to check the forecast ahead of time and pack appropriately. Wearing light, breathable clothing is essential if you're going in the summer, when it can get very hot and muggy. Bring light-colored clothing like linen or cotton, along with comfy dresses, skirts, or shorts. To protect yourself from the sun, it's also a good idea to wear a cap or a wide-brimmed hat in addition to sunscreen and sunglasses. Warmer apparel, such sweaters, long-sleeved shirts, and a high-quality coat or jacket, is essential if you're traveling in the winter. It's also a good idea to bring a scarf, gloves, and a hat to stay warm because Venice can get very cold and wet during the winter. Packing layers that you may add or remove as needed is ideal for spring and fall, when the weather is more erratic. For milder mornings and evenings, a lightweight jacket or cardigan is helpful, but in the event of rain, an umbrella or waterproof jacket is necessary.

Another important item to carry for Venice is footwear. The city is best explored on foot because it is difficult to navigate by any other means due to its narrow streets, bridges, and canals. Given that you will probably be walking a lot during your trip, comfortable walking shoes are essential. Because parts of Venice's streets and bridges can be uneven or slick, especially after rain, wear shoes that are supportive and have decent traction. The city's cobblestone streets and many steps make it impractical to bring shoes with thin soles or high heels. While sturdy shoes or waterproof boots are advised in the winter to keep your feet warm and dry, comfortable sandals or sneakers are a fantastic option if you are traveling in the summer. It's also important to remember that Venice frequently experiences acqua alta, or flooding, especially during the fall and winter. To keep your feet dry while traveling during this time, think about bringing waterproof shoes or boots, or even lightweight rain boots.

Your packing list for Venice should include a number of other necessities in addition to clothes and shoes. Because it eliminates the need to purchase bottled water and keeps you hydrated while visiting the city, a reusable water bottle is an excellent item to have. You can replenish your bottle as needed because Venice has public fountains that provide safe and clean drinking water. When you are out and about, a compact daypack or backpack is also helpful for carrying your belongings, including a guidebook, a map, a water bottle, and any souvenirs you might buy. To make sure your phone stays charged throughout the day, think about packing a portable charger or power bank if you want to use it for navigation or shooting pictures. Since Italy utilizes a different kind of electrical outlet than many other nations, a travel adaptor is also a must. Bring an adaptor that works with Italian outlets and make sure your devices have the correct voltage and plug type.

To save room and prevent overpacking, it's crucial to bring only the essential personal belongings and toiletries. Basic necessities like shampoo, soap, and towels are provided by the majority of hotels and lodgings in Venice, so unless you have particular tastes, you don't need to carry them. Nonetheless, you should bring along any personal belongings you use frequently, such deodorant, toothpaste, a toothbrush, and any prescription drugs you might require. Mosquitoes can be a bother in Venice, particularly in the nights, so it's a good idea to bring insect repellent if you're going there in the summer. Another helpful item is a compact first aid pack, which enables you to treat minor illnesses or accidents without going to a drugstore. Pack supplies like bandages, painkillers, and any more prescription drugs you might require for the journey.

When preparing for Venice, it's also critical to consider the city's particular difficulties. For instance, you will need to carry your bags across stairs and uneven ground due to Venice's canals and bridges, so it is better to pack light and select a suitcase or bag with wheels that are stable and manageable. Select a carry-on size bag if at all possible to save on the trouble of checking bags and to facilitate navigating the city's winding streets. To protect your belongings, think about bringing a money belt or a lockable bag if you are visiting during the busiest time of year, when Venice can get congested. Although pickpocketing is not a big problem in Venice, it is nevertheless advisable to exercise caution, particularly in crowded places like the Rialto Bridge or St. Mark's Square.

Lastly, it's critical to budget for any pre-trip purchases you might need to make, such apparel, shoes, or travel equipment. To prevent overspending, make a list of the things you already own and those you need to get. Then, rank the most important goods first. If you don't want to spend money on items you will just use for this trip, look for specials or discounts on travel gear and think about borrowing items from friends or family. You can make sure you are ready for your vacation to Venice without going over budget by making a list of the things you need to pack and budgeting for them in advance. In addition to saving you money, packing effectively and sensibly will increase the enjoyment of your trip because you will have everything you need to comfortably and easily explore this amazing city.

When organizing a vacation to Venice, two of the most crucial factors to take into account are safety and travel insurance. Even though Venice is a friendly and safe city overall, it's a good idea to be ready for any unforeseen circumstances that can come up while you're there. While adhering to safety precautions guarantees that you may enjoy your trip without needless worry or hassles, travel insurance offers financial protection and peace of mind in the event of crises. You can maximize your time in Venice and concentrate on discovering its beauty, history, and culture by realizing the value of travel insurance and adopting the appropriate safety measures.

Any journey, including one to Venice, requires the purchase of travel insurance. It is intended to shield you from monetary losses and offer support in the event of unanticipated circumstances like medical crises, cancelled trips, misplaced luggage, or delays in your journey. Selecting a travel insurance package that addresses the particular requirements of your journey is crucial. For instance, confirm that the policy covers your pre-existing medical conditions if you have any. A coverage that covers trip disruptions or cancellations due to weather-related concerns should be taken into consideration if you are visiting during the winter, when Venice is vulnerable to flooding (acqua alta). Likewise, be sure your policy covers recreational activities like boating and water sports if you intend to engage in them.

One of the most crucial aspects of travel insurance is medical coverage. Even though Venice has first-rate medical facilities, medical care can be costly, particularly for tourists from outside the EU. You are protected in the event that you become ill or are hurt while traveling if you have medical coverage with your travel insurance. This covers prescription drugs, doctor visits, hospital stays, and emergency medical evacuation. It's also a good idea to always have a copy of your insurance policy and emergency contact information on hand so you can get help fast if you need it. You might qualify for a European Health Insurance Card (EHIC) if you're coming from a European Union nation. This card gives you free or heavily discounted access to public healthcare services in Italy. However, since it does not cover private healthcare, medical evacuation, or other non-medical costs, an EHIC cannot be used in place of travel insurance.

Trip cancellation and interruption coverage is a crucial component of travel insurance. This safeguards you in the event that unanticipated events, including illness, injury, or a family emergency, force you to postpone or cancel your vacation. Additionally, it can pay non-refundable costs including airfare, lodging, and tours. To find out what is and is not covered, thoroughly read the policy terms before buying travel insurance. Selecting an insurance that fits your needs is crucial because some may not cover specific occurrences, such pandemics or natural catastrophes.

Another frequent problem that travel insurance might help with is delayed or lost luggage. Sometimes delays or improper luggage handling result from Venice's unusual transit system, which depends on boats and water taxis. Travel insurance that includes baggage coverage pays for items you might need to buy in case your luggage is delayed, as well as for lost, stolen, or damaged luggage. Packing a carry-on bag with necessities like clothes, toiletries, and prescription drugs reduces the chance of misplaced luggage and ensures you have everything you need in case your checked luggage is delayed.

To guarantee a seamless and pleasurable journey to Venice, it is crucial to adhere to safety precautions in addition to acquiring travel insurance. Being mindful of your surroundings and taking preventative measures to safeguard your possessions are among the most crucial safety advices. Pickpocketing can happen in crowded places like St. Mark's Square, the Rialto Bridge, and on public transit, even though Venice is a generally safe city. Keep your valuables hidden and safe to lower the chance of theft. Don't carry a lot of cash; instead, use a money belt or a zippered crossbody bag to hold your passport, credit cards, and cash. When using an ATM, use caution and pick one that is located in a busy, well-lit area. Consider placing pricey belongings, like jewelry or cameras, in your hotel safe when not in use if you are traveling with them.

Navigating Venice's canals and bridges is another crucial aspect of safety. You will probably walk a lot while visiting Venice because it is a pedestrian city. To prevent slips and falls, it is crucial to wear comfortable and supportive shoes because the streets and bridges can be congested, narrow, and uneven. Walking close to the canals should be done with extra caution because many places lack rails, making it simple to trip and fall into the water. When crossing bridges or strolling close to canals with kids, keep a tight watch on them and hold their hands. Follow the safety advice given by the operators when taking public transit, such as vaporettos or water taxis, and use caution when getting on and off because the boats may move suddenly.

Venice's distinct climate necessitates extra consideration for weather-related safety. Particularly in the fall and winter, when high tides can result in acqua alta, the city is vulnerable to floods. It is crucial to keep up with the tidal levels and weather forecast if you are traveling during this period. While many lodging establishments offer rubber boots for visitors to use in the event of flooding, you might also wish to pack your own waterproof shoes. It can be unsafe to walk in deep or swiftly moving water, therefore heed the local authorities' recommendations. Venice may get hot and muggy in the summer, so it's critical to drink plenty of water and wear sunscreen. To prevent heat exhaustion, wear lightweight clothing, a hat, and sunscreen. You should also take pauses in areas with air conditioning or shade.

Another piece of advice for staying safe in Venice is to use caution when traveling by water. Although gondola trips are a common pastime, it's crucial to select a licensed gondolier to protect your safety. An official license is posted on the gondola of a licensed gondolier, who also wears a uniform. To prevent tipping the boat, pay close attention to the gondolier's instructions and sit down gently before boarding a gondola. Make sure the water taxi you are using is an authorized one and that the boat is marked with the license number. Steer clear of unregistered or unofficial boats as they could not be safe.

Last but not least, having a plan is crucial in an emergency. Prior to your departure, write down crucial phone numbers, including your country's embassy or consulate, the local emergency services, and your travel insurance company. Get help from your embassy or consulate if you misplace your passport or other crucial documents. Do not be afraid to ask for assistance if you need it; many hotels in Venice have staff that can assist you in an emergency. A reliable friend or relative back home should also be given access to your travel schedule so they are aware of your whereabouts and can get in touch with you in an emergency.

You can guarantee a worry-free journey to Venice by getting comprehensive travel insurance and heeding these safety recommendations. Although it is hard to foresee every scenario that could occur, being ready and taking preventative measures will enable you to face any obstacles head-on. Venice is a unique city, and you can concentrate on taking in its history, culture, and beauty while remaining safe and secure during your trip if you plan ahead and are mindful of your surroundings.

CHAPTER 2

TRANSPORTATION OPTION FOR GETTING TO AND AROUND VENICE

Reaching Venice

By Air: Treviso and Marco Polo Airports

One of the most popular ways to start your trip to this remarkable city is to fly into Venice. There are two major airports in Venice: Treviso Airport, which is smaller and mostly used by low-cost carriers, and Marco Polo Airport, which is the main international airport nearer to the city. Although both airports offer access to Venice, their locations, amenities, and modes of transit are different. A seamless and stress-free arrival depends on knowing the specifics of each airport and how to get from there to Venice. The trip from the airport to the city center is different from arriving at most other locations because Venice is a unique city without automobiles or roads. You can make the greatest decisions for your tastes, schedule, and money if you plan ahead and know what to expect.

The primary airport servicing Venice and the surrounding area is Marco Polo Airport, formally known as Venice Marco Polo Airport (VCE). It is located close to the mainland town of Tessera, about 13 kilometers (8 miles) north of Venice. The majority of travelers find this airport to be the most convenient since it is up to date, well-equipped, and handles a lot of domestic and international flights. When you arrive at Marco Polo Airport, you will find a variety of amenities to suit your needs, such as free Wi-Fi, shops, restaurants, baggage storage, ATMs, and currency exchange services. You can easily find your way to the transit options that will take you into Venice because the airport is modest in comparison to major international hubs.

There are a number of ways to get from Marco Polo Airport to Venice, depending on your spending limit and time commitment. Water travel is one of the most well-liked and picturesque ways to get to Venice. Operating straight from the airport, the Alilaguna water bus service transports visitors to the cruise terminal, St. Mark's Square, and the Rialto Bridge, among other locations in Venice. The Alilaguna boats leave at a wharf about ten minutes' walk from the airport terminal, and depending on your destination, the trip into Venice takes between forty-five and an hour. With breathtaking views of the lagoon and the city's famous skyline, this choice is especially alluring since it lets you see Venice from the sea as soon as you get there. For most travelers, the Alilaguna service is a cost-effective choice, and tickets can be bought online ahead of time or at the airport.

Land transportation is an additional means of transportation from Marco Polo Airport to Venice. Regular routes are run by the ATVO and ACTV bus services between the airport and Piazzale Roma, the main bus station and the last location in Venice that can be reached by car. It takes around 20 minutes to go to Piazzale Roma on the ATVO buses, which are air-conditioned and comfortable. In addition to being a dependable and reasonably priced choice, the ACTV buses are a member of the local public transit system and could make extra stops along the route. After reaching Piazzale Roma, you have two options for getting to your destination in Venice: walking or riding a vaporetto, or water bus. It's important to keep in mind that Piazzale Roma provides facilities for storing heavy bags and is conveniently located near other parts of Venice.

Taxis and private transportation are also offered from Marco Polo Airport for individuals who would rather have a more convenient and private option. While water taxis can take you straight to your hotel or other places in Venice, land taxis can take you to Piazzale Roma. Although they are the quickest and most direct route to your location, water taxis are also the priciest choice. Depending on the distance and the number of passengers, a private water taxi ride from the airport to Venice may cost between 100 and 150 euros. Because of the ease and the distinctive experience of arriving in Venice by boat, this alternative can be worth taking into consideration if you are going in a group or have a lot of luggage.

The second airport servicing Venice is Treviso Airport, formally known as Treviso Antonio Canova Airport (TSF). It is located close to the town of Treviso, around 40 kilometers (25 miles) from Venice. Low-cost carriers like Ryanair and Wizz Air are the main users of Treviso Airport, which is significantly smaller than Marco Polo Airport. Due to the cheaper airfare, it is still a well-liked option for low-budget tourists even though it is farther from Venice than Marco Polo Airport. Although there are less amenities at Treviso Airport than at Marco Polo Airport, you may still find standard conveniences including a café, a small store, ATMs, and vehicle rental services. You can easily find your way to the transit alternatives that will take you to Venice on account of the airport's tiny size.

Usually, there is a direct bus service or a bus and train combination to go from Treviso Airport to Venice. Direct buses from Treviso Airport to Venice's Piazzale Roma are run by the ATVO and Barzi bus companies. Tickets can be bought at the airport or online in advance, and the trip takes between 40 and 70 minutes, depending on traffic. The buses are a practical choice for the majority of passengers because they are cozy and include luggage storage. From Treviso Airport, you can take a local bus or cab to the Treviso Centrale train station, which is roughly 3 kilometers (2 miles) away, if you would rather go by rail. From there, you can take a train to the center of Venice, to the Santa Lucia station. Trains run often throughout the day, and the trip takes around 30 minutes. Although this alternative necessitates an extra transfer, it can be a wise decision if you would rather take the train or if the bus schedule does not coincide with your arrival time.

Private transportation from Treviso Airport to Venice are also offered to those who appreciate convenience and are prepared to pay more. While private water taxis can transport you straight to your hotel or other destinations in Venice, private automobile services can transport you to Piazzale Roma. Similar to Marco Polo Airport, private water taxis are the priciest choice, but they have the benefit of providing individualized and direct service. This can be a good choice if you have a lot of luggage or are going in a group.

To prevent confusion or delays, it's crucial to arrange your transportation to Venice in advance, regardless of the airport you land at. When selecting the ideal alternative for your trip, take into account elements like your budget, the quantity of luggage you are carrying, and the location of your lodging. Verify if the hotel you are staying at has a shuttle service or can make travel arrangements for you. Since not all services take credit cards, it's also a good idea to have some euros on hand for other costs like transportation.

Traveling by flight to Venice marks the start of an incredible adventure to one of the world's most distinctive and stunning cities. Knowing your alternatives for transportation and making advance plans can guarantee a seamless and pleasurable beginning to your journey, regardless of whether you land at Marco Polo Airport or Treviso Airport. The allure and enchantment of Venice start as soon as you arrive, and you may maximize your experience right away if you prepare properly.

By Train: Santa Lucia Station in Venice

One of the most practical and picturesque ways to get into this remarkable city is via rail. Stazione di Venezia Santa Lucia, often known as Venice Santa Lucia Station, is the city's major train station and the point of entry for passengers arriving by rail. This station, which is located exactly on the Grand Canal, provides a smooth journey from the mainland to the center of Venice, enabling guests to enter the city's distinct and alluring ambiance right away. Arriving by train is a convenient and effective way to avoid making extra transfers from the mainland, whether you are traveling from inside Italy or from another European nation. A seamless and pleasurable arrival depends on knowing the specifics of Venice Santa Lucia Station, the services it provides, and how to get from the station to your final destination.

The only train station in Venice is Venice Santa Lucia Station, which is located on the western outskirts of the old city. This is a significant distinction because there is another station on the mainland called Venezia Mestre. Although Mestre is outside of Venice's lagoon, it is frequently utilized as a stopover for tourists en route to the city. When purchasing train tickets to Venice, it is important to make sure that the destination listed on the ticket is "Venezia Santa Lucia," as this will take you straight to the heart of the city. You can save time and effort by arriving at Santa Lucia Station, which eliminates the need for additional transportation to get to Venice.

The station itself is a contemporary, orderly establishment that serves the requirements of both domestic and foreign passengers. Although it is easy to traverse due to its tiny size in comparison to major European rail stations, it nonetheless has all the necessary amenities. Train tickets can be bought or picked up from ticket counters and self-service kiosks located within the station. You can also use these services to purchase tickets for subsequent trains if you plan to continue your travel after visiting Venice. In addition to a few cafés and restaurants where you may have a bite to eat or a cup of coffee, the station features a variety of stores and kiosks offering snacks, beverages, and travel necessities. If you need to take out cash or exchange money when you are there, there are also ATMs and currency exchange services accessible.

The fact that Venice Santa Lucia Station is located right on the Grand Canal is among its most significant qualities. A stunning view of the canal, complete with its recognizable gondolas, water taxis, and old buildings bordering the water's edge, greets you as soon as you exit the station. One of the reasons traveling by train is such a great experience is the instantaneous immersion into Venice's distinctive atmosphere. Because the station is close to several well-known sites and has good access to Venice's public transit system, it's also a great place to start your exploration of the city.

Although it is quite easy to go from Venice Santa Lucia Station to your lodging or other locations in the city, Venice's unusual layout does necessitate some preparation. Since there are no roads or cars in the city, people must travel by foot or boat. Operating on the Grand Canal and other waterways, the vaporetto, or water bus, is one of the most well-liked modes of transportation in Venice. It is simple to board a boat and get to your destination because the vaporetto stops right in front of Santa Lucia Station at the Ferrovia stop. Frequent water buses travel a number of routes across the city, stopping at important sites such the Rialto Bridge, St. Mark's Square, and the islands of Murano and Burano. You can buy tickets for the vaporetto at the ticket machines beside the water bus stops or at the ACTV ticket office inside the station. Buying a travel card that permits unlimited rides for a predetermined amount of time—such as 24, 48, or 72 hours—is typically more economical, particularly if you intend to use the vaporetto frequently while visiting.

Water taxis are also offered at Santa Lucia Station if you'd rather take a more direct and private route. You can go straight to your hotel or other places in Venice using these motorboats. Compared to the vaporetto, water taxis are quicker and more practical, but they cost a lot more. A water taxi ride usually costs between 60 and 100 euros, depending on the distance and the number of passengers. Because of its ease, a water taxi might be a suitable choice if you are traveling with a large group of people or have a lot of luggage. Notably, water taxis are available twenty-four hours a day and can be reserved in advance or rented on the spot.

Santa Lucia Station is a great place to start if you want to explore Venice on foot. Many of the city's major attractions are accessible by foot from the station, while the city itself is comparatively tiny and compact. For instance, it takes roughly 20 minutes to walk from Santa Lucia to the Rialto Bridge, and 30 to 40 minutes to walk from St. Mark's Square. Walking in Venice is a unique experience because you will have to traverse charming bridges, navigate winding alleyways, and come across secret squares and waterways. However, it is vital to be prepared for the problems of walking in Venice, such as uneven ground, stairs, and crowds, especially during the peak tourist season. Comfortable shoes and a good map or navigation program are important for getting around on foot.

It is important to keep in mind that due to Venice's lack of highways and automobiles, you will have to wheel or carry your big baggage across bridges and cobblestone streets. Use baggage with strong wheels and pack light to make this easy. As an alternative, you can pay for a porter service, which can deliver your bags to your lodging and is offered at Santa Lucia Station. If you have trouble lugging heavy bags or your hotel is far from the station, this service may be quite useful.

The train ride itself is frequently the highlight of a trip for people traveling to Venice from other regions of Italy or Europe. Major towns like Rome, Florence, Milan, and Bologna, as well as foreign locations like Paris, Munich, and Vienna, are all easily accessible from Venice. With features like air conditioning, Wi-Fi, and onboard refreshments, Trenitalia and Italo's high-speed trains offer quick and comfortable service to Venice. The train traverses the lagoon on a lengthy causeway in the last portion of the trip to Venice, providing breathtaking views of the city and the water beyond. Setting the tone for your trip, this method of getting to Venice is an unforgettable experience.

A smooth and delightful way to start your trip to this enchanted city is by arriving at Venice Santa Lucia Station. For passengers arriving by train, the station is a perfect starting

point because of its convenient location, state-of-the-art amenities, and first-rate transit connections. The travel from the station to the city is easy and uncomplicated, enabling you to immediately begin taking in Venice's beauty and charm whether you decide to continue by vaporetto, water taxi, or foot. You may guarantee a stress-free and unforgettable beginning to your stay in Venice by organizing your arrival in advance and becoming acquainted with the options available.
Parking Options Outside the City for Cars

Since Venice is not like most other cities in the world, driving there is a unique experience. There are no highways or automobiles in the city itself, and the historic heart of Venice is located on a group of islands in a lagoon. As a result, if you are driving to Venice, you will have to park your car outside of the city and proceed by foot or boat. To guarantee a seamless and stress-free beginning to your stay, it is crucial to comprehend the parking options accessible and to properly organize your arrival. On the mainland and on the outskirts of the city, Venice offers a number of parking lots, each with unique benefits and things to keep in mind. The length of your stay, your budget, and how near you want to be to the city center all play a role in selecting the best parking choice.

The two primary locations where cars can be parked close to the city are Piazzale Roma and Tronchetto, which offer the most practical parking choices for tourists arriving in Venice by car. The nearest location to the historic center that may be reached by car is Piazzale Roma. The Ponte della Libertà, a lengthy bridge that across the lagoon, connects this expansive piazza at the edge of Venice to the mainland. Before reaching Venice's pedestrian-only zones, Piazzale Roma is the last destination for taxis, buses, and autos. For those who wish to be as close to the city center as possible, parking at Piazzale Roma is perfect because it makes it easy to go to the vaporetto (water bus) stops, water taxis, or even your lodging if it's close by. However, because Piazzale Roma is so close to the center, parking there is also the most expensive alternative. The Autorimessa Comunale and the Garage San Marco are Piazzale Roma's primary parking lots. Both are open around-the-clock and provide multi-level, safe parking. Since these facilities can fill up quickly, it is strongly advised to reserve a parking spot in advance, particularly during the busiest travel seasons.

Another well-liked parking choice for tourists arriving in Venice by automobile is Tronchetto. Slightly more distant from the city than Piazzale Roma, Tronchetto is located on an artificial island just west of the old center and has cheaper parking. For those who don't mind a little further drive to get to the city center, the Tronchetto Parking Garage is a fantastic option because it's a big, contemporary facility with plenty of room for cars. The People Mover is an automated tram that runs from Tronchetto to Piazzale Roma, and it takes only a few minutes to get there. The People Mover is a great way to get from Tronchetto to the city because it is cheap and runs often. As an alternative, you can travel to Venice from Tronchetto via water taxi or vaporetto. Due to its proximity, Tronchetto parking is also a fantastic choice for visitors who intend to take a cruise from the Venice Cruise Terminal.

There are a number of parking lots in Mestre, the mainland neighborhood that is connected to Venice by the Ponte della Libertà, for people who would rather park on the mainland and avoid driving into Venice entirely. For tourists on a tight budget or those who do not want quick access to the city center, parking in Mestre is sometimes less expensive than that at Piazzale Roma or Tronchetto. There are several parking alternatives in Mestre, such as open-air spaces and safe garages. The Parcheggio Saba Venezia Mestre and the Venezia Mestre Station Parking are two of Mestre's most well-liked parking lots. You can go to Venice by tram, bus, or train from Mestre. It just takes ten to fifteen minutes to travel by train from Venezia Mestre Station to Venezia Santa Lucia Station. Piazzale Roma is often served by buses and trams, making it simple to get from Mestre to Venice.

Using one of the park-and-ride lots close to the Ponte della Libertà entrance is an additional way to find parking on the mainland. These establishments, like the Park San Giuliano, have reasonably priced parking and excellent public transportation connections to Venice. The Park San Giuliano offers shuttle bus service to Piazzale Roma and is located in a sizable green space. For those who wish to have easy access to the city without paying the higher parking costs at Piazzale Roma and Tronchetto, this alternative is especially practical.

The duration of your stay and the degree of convenience you need should be taken into account when selecting a parking option for your trip to Venice. Despite the increased price, parking at Piazzale Roma or Tronchetto can be the best option if you are only visiting Venice for a day or two and want to make the most of your time there. However, parking in Mestre or at a park-and-ride on the mainland can save you money if you are traveling on a tight budget or are planning a longer stay. Before choosing, it is a good idea to inquire with your lodging because some hotels in Venice provide parking packages or discounts at specific garages.

It's crucial to arrange your arrival ahead of time and become acquainted with the route to the parking facility of your choice, regardless of where you decide to park. Allow extra time for traffic and navigation because the highways leading to Venice can be congested, particularly during the busiest travel seasons. In order to avoid confusion, if you are using a GPS or navigation software, be careful to enter the address of your parking facility instead than just "Venice." It will be easier to leave if you note the location of your parking facility and any instructions for getting your car when you get there.

Compared to other forms of transportation, driving to Venice involves more preparation, but it can be a flexible and convenient alternative, particularly if you are coming from other regions of Italy or Europe. You can guarantee a hassle-free beginning to your stay by being aware of the parking alternatives available and selecting the one that best meets your needs. With the correct planning, you may start your trip with confidence and ease and discover all of Venice's charm and beauty.

Getting Around the Lagoon

Gondolas, Vaporetto (Water Bus), and Water Taxis

Venice is unlike any other city in the world, so getting there and exploring its lagoon is a genuinely unique experience. Venice, which is made up of a number of islands connected by bridges and canals, lacks highways and automobiles; all forms of transit are done on foot or by boat. This implies that everyone traveling to Venice must know how to navigate the lagoon. Water taxis, vaporettos (water buses), and gondolas are the primary forms of transportation in the city; each has a unique function and provides a unique experience. You can get to your lodging, see the city's sights, or just take in the atmosphere of this enchanted location more effectively and joyfully if you know how these alternatives operate, how much they cost, and when to use them.

One of the most opulent and practical ways to go around Venice is by water taxi. These are private motorboats that transport people straight to their destination, much like a regular taxi. If you are traveling with heavy suitcases, water taxis are especially helpful because they can transport you straight to your hotel or other places with private docks, sparing you the trouble of dragging your things over the city's numerous bridges and through its winding streets. Because they are quicker and more direct than other modes of transportation, they are also a fantastic choice if you are pressed for time and need to go somewhere fast. Water taxis are available at certain locations all across the city, especially at important entry points like Venice Santa Lucia Station, Piazzale Roma, and Marco Polo Airport. Additionally, you can reserve a water taxi in advance online or through your hotel, which is particularly useful at peak times when demand is strong.

Water taxis are the priciest form of transportation in Venice, notwithstanding their convenience. The distance, the number of passengers, and the time of day all affect how much a water taxi costs, but for a quick trip within the city, charges usually start at about 60 to 70 euros. Additional fees could be incurred for additional stops along the route, luggage, or overnight service. The cost can be split among passengers if you are going in a group, which lowers the cost. However, water taxis might not be the most sensible choice for budget-conscious or lone visitors. In order to avoid any surprises, it is advisable to check the fare with the driver before beginning your trip, as water taxis are not metered.

The primary mode of public transportation in Venice is the vaporetto, or water bus, which is utilized by both residents and visitors to navigate the city and the nearby islands. The vaporetto network, which is run by the ACTV, connects important landmarks, residential areas, and islands including Murano, Burano, and Lido via the Grand Canal, smaller canals, and the lagoon. Similar to a city bus system, the vaporettos are big, motorized boats that can accommodate a lot of people. They run on a set timetable with defined stops. One of the most economical and useful methods to get around

Venice is via vaporetto, particularly if you intend to visit numerous different places or spend several days there.

Tickets for the vaporetto can be bought online, in ticket offices, or at vending machines. It's crucial to scan your ticket at the machines at the vaporetto stops to confirm it before boarding. Although a single ticket costs about 9.50 euros and lasts for 75 minutes, buying a travel pass is more economical if you want to ride the vaporetto frequently. Travel passes allow unlimited rides during their validity term and are available for 24, 48, or 72 hours, as well as extended periods. A 24-hour pass, for instance, costs about 25 euros, whereas a 72-hour pass costs about 65 euros. For those who wish to see the city and its islands without having to buy separate tickets for each trip, these passes are a fantastic choice.

Although it is quite easy to manage the system because the vaporetto routes are numbered and color-coded, it is still a good idea to become familiar with the schedules and route map before departing. The most well-traveled route is Line 1, which follows the Grand Canal and makes stops at several of Venice's most well-known sites, such as the Accademia, the Rialto Bridge, and St. Mark's Square. Due to its many stops, this route is slower than others, but it provides a beautiful and leisurely way to see the city. If you need to go somewhere fast, Line 2 is a fantastic option because it is quicker and makes fewer stops while still traveling along the Grand Canal. Line 12, which connects Murano, Burano, and Torcello, is one of the several routes that link to the outer islands. Because certain lines run in a loop or have restricted service at particular times of the day, it is crucial to use the vaporetto with awareness of the direction of travel and the precise stops served by each route.

Possibly the most recognizable image of Venice, gondolas are a must-see for many tourists. Gondoliers, who use a single oar to navigate the canals, have been operating these classic, handcrafted boats in Venice for generations. Gondola rides are a romantic and leisurely method to take in the city's beauty and charm rather than a useful form of transportation. Usually lasting between thirty and forty minutes, a gondola ride offers a different view of the city than you would receive from the Grand Canal or on foot. It takes you through some of Venice's smaller, quieter canals. To enhance the experience, many gondoliers often sing or offer comments while the journey is underway.

The city sets the price of gondola rides, which typically start at about 80 euros for a half-hour ride during the day and 100 euros for a ride after 7:00 PM. If you are traveling with friends, you can split the cost because these rates include the entire gondola, which can hold up to six passengers. Longer rides or special requests, such a serenade, can incur additional fees. Although gondola rides are not inexpensive, many tourists view them as the high point of their trip because they offer a distinctive and unforgettable way to see Venice. Gondola stations are located all around the city, especially close to well-known tourist destinations like St. Mark's Square and the Rialto Bridge, if you're interested in taking a ride.

Planning your routes and modes of transportation in advance is crucial while crossing Venice's lagoon, particularly if you're going during the busiest traffic times when vaporettos and water taxis can get packed. When choosing a mode of transportation, take into account elements like your spending limit, where you plan to stay, and the destinations you wish to see. For instance, the vaporetto is perhaps the most practical and economical choice if you are staying close to the Grand Canal and intend to see the main sites. Given its speed and convenience, a water taxi can be worth the additional expense if you are visiting one of the outer islands or have a limited amount of time. Additionally, a gondola trip is the ideal option if all you want is a romantic and relaxed encounter.

An integral part of Venice's allure and a singular experience of traveling to this remarkable location is navigating its lagoon. You can make the most of your time in Venice and appreciate the ride just as much as the final destination by learning how gondolas, vaporettos, and water taxis operate. You can easily explore the city's canals and islands and make priceless memories of your stay in this enchanted location with a little forethought and preparation.

Walking in Venice

One of the most satisfying and unusual things a tourist can do in Venice is to go for a walk. Since vehicles, buses, and bicycles are not permitted in the old center, Venice is a pedestrian haven unlike most other cities in the world. Built on a system of islands connected by more than 400 bridges and canals, the city is a labyrinth of squares, alleyways, and narrow streets that are best explored on foot. Walking is a vital component of taking in Venice's charm, history, and beauty; it's not just a means of transportation. Whether it's a secret courtyard, a serene waterway, or a building that dates back centuries and has elaborate embellishments, Venice offers something new at every turn. It is essential to comprehend the layout of the city, how to get around its streets, and what to anticipate when you visit this remarkable location if you want to enjoy walking in Venice to the fullest.

Particularly for tourists accustomed to grid-like towns, Venice's layout may initially appear perplexing. San Marco, Cannaregio, Castello, Dorsoduro, San Polo, and Santa Croce are the six "sestieri" that make up Venice. Together, the sestieres make up Venice's historic center, each with its own unique personality and charms. The sestieri are separated into two major sections by the Grand Canal, the city's principal canal, which forms an S-shape as it passes through the heart of Venice. The Rialto Bridge, the Accademia Bridge, the Scalzi Bridge (by the train station), and the contemporary Constitution Bridge (by Piazzale Roma) are the only four bridges that span the Grand Canal. These bridges link the various sections of Venice and offer access to significant locations, making them essential landmarks for city navigation.

When wandering around Venice, one of the first things to realize is that the streets aren't always clear-cut. Numerous streets are winding and tiny, and as you go from one neighborhood to another, they sometimes change names. Venice also contains a lot of dead ends, where a street may lead to a canal that cannot be crossed by a bridge. This may make it difficult to navigate, particularly for inexperienced users. Nonetheless, getting lost in Venice is frequently regarded as a part of the experience since it enables you to find calm areas and secret treasures that you may not have otherwise discovered. Venice features a system of directional indicators painted on building walls to aid in navigation. Major landmarks including "San Marco," "Rialto," and "Ferrovia" (the train station) are indicated by these markers. Even without a map or navigation app, you may still find your way around the city by following these signs.

The majority of Venice's major attractions are within walking distance of one another, despite the city's labyrinthine architecture. For instance, the walk from the train station to St. Mark's Square takes roughly half an hour, while the walk from the Rialto Bridge to St. Mark's Square takes about twenty minutes. In addition to being useful, walking in Venice is fun since there is stunning architecture, historical sites, and scenic views everywhere you look. You will encounter innumerable bridges along the way, each with its own distinct style and personality. While some bridges are elaborate and adorned with statues or carvings, others are straightforward and practical. Crossing the bridges serves as a reminder of Venice's connection to the water and is an essential component of its allure.

When traveling around Venice, one of the most crucial things to remember is that the streets and bridges can be uneven, with cobblestones, steps, and slopes that can be difficult for certain tourists to navigate. Given that you will probably be walking for extended amounts of time and navigating a variety of terrain, comfortable shoes with adequate support are crucial. Since they can make it difficult to walk on the uneven streets and traverse the numerous bridges, high heels and thin sandals are not advised. It's crucial to think about how you'll carry your luggage if you're traveling with it, since you could have to carry it over bridges or up and down stairs. To make moving about the city easier, many tourists opt to bring lightweight bags or luggage with strong wheels.

The crowds are another thing to consider when walking around Venice, particularly during the busiest travel times. It can be challenging to find a peaceful place or move swiftly in crowded places like St. Mark's Square, the Rialto Bridge, and the streets around the Grand Canal. Consider visiting Venice early in the morning or late at night, when the streets are less crowded and the city has a more tranquil feel. In order to see a more genuine side of Venice and take your time exploring the city, you can also go off the usual route to less-traveled locations like Cannaregio or Castello.

Venice's many hidden gems, such as its tiny churches, art galleries, neighborhood stores, and cafés, can be found by strolling throughout the city. Narrow streets and tunnels abound in the city, leading to surprising locations like a serene courtyard, a quaint square, or a canal with a breathtaking outlook. These undiscovered locations offer a window into Venetian daily life and are frequently less crowded than the major tourist destinations. Spend some time observing the buildings' intricate details as you explore, such as the elaborate windows, balconies, and carvings that showcase Venice's rich cultural heritage.

Navigating the city's high tides, or "acqua alta," is one of the difficulties of walking in Venice. During high tide, parts of the city, such as St. Mark's Square, can flood, making it difficult to walk in some places. To prevent pedestrians from getting wet during acqua alta, the city has a system of elevated walkways in place. If you are traveling in the fall or winter, when high tides are more frequent, it is a good idea to check the tide forecast before you go and to pack waterproof shoes or boots.

In addition to being a useful mode of transportation, walking in Venice is a must-do activity for taking in the city's distinct personality and allure. It is best enjoyed on foot because of the tranquil and timeless environment created by the lack of traffic and the presence of water. You will experience a sense of wonder at Venice's beauty and inventiveness as well as a connection to its history and culture. Walking in Venice is an amazing experience that lets you fully immerse yourself in this remarkable city, whether you're exploring the busy streets surrounding St. Mark's Square, meandering through the serene alleys of Cannaregio, or crossing a bridge with a view of the Grand Canal. You can easily navigate Venice's streets and canals and experience the beauty that makes it one of the world's most distinctive travel destinations if you are prepared and have a spirit of adventure.

Advice for a Stress-Free Arrival

It's thrilling to arrive in Venice, but to guarantee a seamless start to your trip, it's crucial to be well-prepared. With its distinctive network of canals, bridges, and winding alleyways, Venice is a city unlike any other. For those who are not familiar with its topography, this can be a problem. Furthermore, Venice, one of the most visited places on earth, has its share of tourist traps, especially at the main entrances like the train station, Piazzale Roma, and the airport. The quality of your arrival and your entire stay in the city can be much improved by knowing how to steer clear of these dangers and how to handle your luggage in Venice's unique setting. You can easily traverse Venice's entry points and get your trip off to a good start with careful planning and attention to detail.

One of the first things to be aware of when arriving in Venice is the possibility for tourist traps at key entry points. These are areas where large numbers of visitors arrive, such as Venice Santa Lucia Station, Marco Polo Airport, Piazzale Roma, and the Tronchetto parking area. Inaccurate information, aggressive sales techniques, or expensive services are common examples of tourist traps that might surprise unprepared tourists. People may offer to carry your bags or lead you to your destination for a price, for instance, at the train station or Piazzale Roma. While some of these services may be real, others can be costly or unneeded, especially if you are capable of handling your luggage and navigating the city on your own. It is crucial to plan your arrival ahead of time and understand exactly how you will go to your lodging or next location in order to avoid slipping into these pitfalls.

Water taxis, a practical but pricey mode of transportation in Venice, are a frequent tourist trap. You can be accosted by people selling expensive private water taxi services at entry locations like the train station or the airport. Water taxis can be a wonderful choice for people who need to get somewhere fast or who have a lot of luggage, but it's crucial to know the regular costs and make reservations through the proper channels whenever you can. To prevent unforeseen fees, ask the driver the fare before boarding if you choose to take a water taxi. As an alternative, think about using the vaporetto, or water bus, which is more dependable and reasonably priced for most passengers. Because the vaporetto follows set routes and timetables, it's simple to plan your trip ahead of time and save money.

Purchasing tickets for transportation is another place where tourists may run into scams. Vendors selling vaporetto tickets or other services at exorbitant costs may be found at key access points. Always buy your tickets from authorized online platforms, ticket offices, or vending machines to avoid spending too much. A travel pass, which provides unlimited rides for a predetermined amount of time and can save you money as compared to buying individual tickets, is something to think about if you want to use public transportation frequently during your visit. Since ticket inspections are frequent in Venice, always careful to verify your ticket before boarding the vaporetto to avoid penalties.

Avoiding tourist traps is important, but so is getting ready for Venice's unusual topography, which can be difficult for visitors carrying large or heavy bags. Bicycles, buses, and cars are not permitted in the city's historic core, which is completely pedestrianized. This implies that you will have to wheel or carry your bags over bridges, through little streets, and occasionally up and down steps. The steps on many of Venice's bridges can be challenging to negotiate while carrying heavy or bulky goods. Packing light and selecting luggage that is manageable in this setting can help your arrival go as smoothly as possible.

Because you will probably need to drag your luggage over uneven floors and cobblestone streets, choose a suitcase or bag with a solid handle and wheels for your vacation to Venice. Due to the uneven topography of Venice, luggage with small or fragile wheels should be avoided. Use a backpack or a smaller, lighter suitcase that you can carry if necessary, if at all possible. Since you might have to walk for 15 to 20 minutes or longer to get to your destination, it's especially vital to pack light if your lodging is far from the main entry points. Remember that Venice's streets may get crowded, especially during the busiest travel seasons, so it will be simpler to move around crowded areas if your luggage is small and easy to handle.

Services are provided to assist in getting bags to your lodging if you are a traveler with large luggage or limited mobility. Major entry points like the train station or Piazzale Roma are good places to engage porter services, such those provided by Cooperativa Trasbagagli. These services can be a practical choice if you are unable to carry your bags alone because they employ carts to move them around the city. To prevent any misconceptions, it is crucial to verify the cost and the estimated time of delivery prior to utilizing these services. It is worthwhile to check with your lodging in advance because certain hotels in Venice can also arrange for a porter to meet you at your arrival location or offer luggage transport services. Carefully planning your approach to your lodging is another piece of advice for handling luggage in Venice. Determine the most direct route using a map or navigation tool, and make a note of any bridges or other impediments you encounter. If you're coming by bus or train, find out if you can walk from your hotel to the station or if you'll need to take a water taxi or vaporetto. If you're taking public transit, be sure you know the route number and the closest vaporetto stop to your lodging. Knowing this ahead of time will help you arrive with less worry and save time.

In case your primary luggage is delayed or difficult to reach, it is also a good idea to have a compact daypack or bag with your basics, like cash, travel documents, and an extra set of clothes. If you are flying into Venice and need to make a transfer from the airport to the city, this is especially crucial. Even if your luggage is not available right away, having a daypack guarantees that you have everything you need for the first day of your trip and gives you more mobility.

Lastly, be ready for the potential of "acqua alta," or high tides, which might happen in the fall and winter. Certain areas of the city, including important entrances like St. Mark's Square, may flood during high tides. To prevent water damage to your things, if you are traveling during this period, think about putting them in waterproof bags and wearing waterproof shoes or boots. It is crucial to be ready for the conditions, even if the city offers elevated paths to assist walkers in navigating flooded regions during acqua alta.

If you take the time to plan ahead and are ready for the particular difficulties that Venice presents, your arrival might be easy and pleasurable. You may start your vacation with confidence and concentrate on taking in the beauty and charm of this remarkable place if you steer clear of tourist traps, pack light, and know how to negotiate Venice's landscape. Arriving in Venice prepared will set the stage for a stress-free and unforgettable trip.

CHAPTER 3

PLACES TO STAY IN VENICE

Selecting the Appropriate Neighborhood

San Marco: Venice's Center

One of the most crucial considerations you will make while organizing your trip is the area in Venice to stay in. Venice is divided into various neighborhoods, each with its own unique personality, ambiance, and benefits. Geographically and historically, San Marco is the most prominent of these being the center of Venice. With some of Venice's most renowned structures, such as St. Mark's Basilica, the Doge's Palace, and the busy St. Mark's Square, it is the most well-known and iconic area in the city. Unmatched proximity to the city's top attractions and the opportunity to experience the lively spirit of Venice's most central and historic district are two benefits of staying in San Marco. To decide if this area is the best option for your stay, it's crucial to comprehend its distinctive features, including both its benefits and possible drawbacks.

With good cause, San Marco is frequently referred to as Venice's throbbing heart. Located on the southern bank of the Grand Canal and bounded by the districts of Castello, San Polo, and Dorsoduro, it is the most central neighborhood in the city. Since many of Venice's most well-known attractions are easily accessible on foot, its central location makes it the perfect starting point for exploring the city. One of the most recognizable public areas in the world, St. Mark's Square, also known as Piazza San Marco, serves as the neighborhood's center. This large plaza, which is a center of activity day and night, is encircled by historic structures like as the Doge's Palace, St. Mark's Basilica, and the Campanile (bell tower). When you stay in San Marco, you can leave your lodging and enter this lively and historic area, with the most well-known sites in the city only a short stroll away.

The convenience that comes with staying in San Marco is one of its key benefits. San Marco, Venice's most central area, offers quick access to both the city's transportation system and its primary attractions. Traveling to other areas of the city and the nearby islands is made simple by the neighborhood's excellent connections to vaporetto (water bus) services, which stop along the Grand Canal and close to St. Mark's Square. Staying in San Marco lets you get the most out of your trip without having to spend too much time driving between places, which is ideal if you are only in Venice for a short time or want to see as much as possible. The neighborhood's central location makes it an ideal starting place for seeing the city, and several of Venice's main attractions, including the Peggy Guggenheim Collection, the Accademia Gallery, and the Rialto Bridge, are all within walking distance of San Marco.

Apart from its practicality, San Marco provides a distinctive and remarkable ambiance. With its charming squares, old buildings, and winding lanes, the area is rich in culture and history and exudes timeless beauty. Grand palaces, quaint lanes, and scenic canals may all be found in San Marco, along with a wide range of stores, eateries, and cafés. The neighborhood surrounding St. Mark's Square is especially bustling, with musicians, artists, and street entertainers contributing to the lively ambiance. San Marco is a great option for tourists who wish to be right in the middle of the activity because it lets you experience Venice's vitality and charm at its most famous.

However, before choosing to stay in San Marco, you should think about the possible difficulties. San Marco is the busiest and most crowded area in Venice, despite being the most well-known and central. The area surrounding St. Mark's Square may get very congested during the busiest travel season, with lots of people crammed into the squares and streets. Navigating the region may become challenging as a result, particularly if you are carrying luggage or have mobility issues. Additionally, especially in the middle of the day when the area is busiest, the crowds might take away from the peaceful atmosphere that many tourists associate with Venice. You could wish to stay in a less central district and go to San Marco in the early morning or late evening, when there are fewer tourists, if you want a calmer and more laid-back ambiance.

The price of lodging in San Marco should also be taken into account. One of the priciest places to stay in Venice is San Marco, which is also the most sought-after neighborhood. This area of the city typically has more expensive hotels, guesthouses, and vacation rentals than other areas, especially if they are close to St. Mark's Square or have views of the Grand Canal. Although there are a few inexpensive options, they might not be many, and in order to receive the best deals, reservations should be made well in advance. While still conveniently close to San Marco, neighboring neighborhoods like Cannaregio or Santa Croce can provide more reasonably priced lodging if you're on a limited budget.

It's important to keep in mind that, in addition to the price, San Marco's central location may result in less local authenticity than other Venice areas. Numerous stores, eateries, and cafés in the vicinity of St. Mark's Square are mostly aimed toward tourists rather than inhabitants. Although this can be useful for locating well-known facilities and services, it can not offer the same feeling of community and local culture as areas like Castello or Cannaregio. If seeing the real Venice is important to you, you might opt to stay in a less crowded neighborhood and include a visit to San Marco in your itinerary.

For many tourists, especially those who are visiting Venice for the first time or have little time to explore the city, San Marco is still a great option in spite of these difficulties. The district provides a singular opportunity to fully immerse oneself in the heart of Venice and is a remarkable and convenient destination to stay due to its central location, historic value, and lively atmosphere. To get the most out of your time in San Marco, think about booking lodging a little bit away from the more crowded locations, such the streets surrounding St. Mark's Square, so you can have a more tranquil and laid-back experience while still being close to the major sights.

Additionally, when the crowds are smaller and the environment is more tranquil, visit the area in the early morning and late evening.

San Marco is a neighborhood that has plenty to offer everyone and offers the opportunity to see Venice at its most famous and historic. San Marco is a destination that embodies Venice and offers a remarkable backdrop for your stay, regardless of whether you are drawn to it by its imposing landmarks, its central location, or its vibrant atmosphere. You can make an informed choice and make sure your Venice lodging satisfies your requirements and expectations by being aware of the benefits and drawbacks of staying in this area. San Marco is a neighborhood that perfectly captures the charm of Venice and provides visitors from all over the world with an experience they won't soon forget because of its fascinating history, breathtaking architecture, and lively energy.

Cannaregio: Genuine and Economical

Since every region of Venice offers a unique experience, choose the ideal district for your lodging is an essential element of trip preparation. Cannaregio is a great choice for tourists looking for a less expensive and more genuine option. One of the biggest and most populous neighborhoods in Venice's north, Cannaregio is renowned for its laid-back vibe, historical significance, and local character. With its peaceful alleyways, traditional stores, and family-run eateries, Cannaregio offers a look into the daily lives of Venetians, in contrast to more tourist-heavy neighborhoods like San Marco. For tourists who wish to see the genuine Venice without going over budget, this district is the perfect starting point because it blends affordability and authenticity. You can determine whether Cannaregio is the ideal neighborhood for your visit by knowing what it has to offer and what to anticipate while staying there.

One of Venice's oldest neighborhoods, Cannaregio's past is intricately linked to the growth of the city. The Venetian Ghetto, a historic Jewish neighborhood that dates back to the 16th century and is still a significant cultural and historical landmark, is located there. With its synagogues, museums, and traditional Jewish bakeries, the Ghetto is an intriguing neighborhood to explore and provides a distinctive look at Venice's rich cultural legacy. When you stay in Cannaregio, you can take in the neighborhood's calmer, more relaxed environment while still immersing yourself in its rich history. Cannaregio is a fantastic option for those who want a slower pace and a more local experience because it feels more domestic and less congested than the busy streets of San Marco.

The affordability of lodging in Cannaregio is one of its key benefits. Cannaregio has more affordable lodging alternatives, including as modest hotels, guesthouses, and vacation rentals, than Venice's more central areas, like San Marco and Dorsoduro. This makes it a desirable option for tourists looking to cut costs on hotel while yet being close to the city's top attractions. You may interact with local hosts and discover more about Venetian culture at several of the family-run lodging options in Cannaregio, which offer a cozy and friendly setting. Additionally, you may eat classic Venetian cuisine without going over budget because the neighborhood's restaurants and cafés are typically more affordable than those in the tourist-heavy districts.

Another important element that makes Cannaregio a fantastic place to stay is its location. With numerous vaporetto (water bus) stops along the Grand Canal and the northern lagoon, the neighborhood has excellent access to the rest of Venice. This facilitates access to various areas of the city, including well-known sites like the islands of Murano and Burano, the Rialto Bridge, and St. Mark's Square. Additionally, Cannaregio is ideally located close to Piazzale Roma, the city's main bus terminal, and Venice Santa Lucia Station, the city's principal train station. Staying in Cannaregio if you are traveling to Venice by rail or bus will allow you to get to your lodging fast and conveniently without having to carry bulky bags across the city's winding streets and bridges. Travelers with limited mobility or those who are visiting Venice for the first time may especially benefit from this.

Cannaregio maintains a feeling of peace and authenticity that distinguishes it from the more crowded parts of Venice, even though it is close to the city's main entrances. Wide canals, peaceful squares, and winding alleyways define the neighborhood, making it ideal for leisurely walks and off-the-beaten-path exploration. You will find hidden treasures like little churches, artisan stores, and neighborhood markets as you explore Cannaregio, where you can get a taste of Venetian daily life. After a day of sightseeing, the neighborhood's laid-back vibe makes it a fantastic spot to rest, and the absence of big crowds makes it possible to have a more private and tranquil experience of Venice.

The chance to experience Cannaregio's thriving food and drink culture is one of the best parts about visiting. You may try regional favorites like cicchetti (small dishes), fresh seafood, and risotto at the neighborhood's many traditional osterias, trattorias, and bacari (Venetian wine bars). Since many of these places are frequented by people rather than visitors, you may savor real Venetian food in a more casual and laid-back atmosphere. Numerous cafés and restaurants along the Fondamenta della Misericordia and Fondamenta degli Ormesini provide a perfect spot to have a drink and mingle with locals and other tourists, making Cannaregio famous for its vibrant nightlife. Cannaregio has something for every taste and price range, whether you're searching for a laid-back supper, a romantic dinner, or a fun night out.

Cannaregio has excellent food options, but it's also a fantastic place to shop. You can buy one-of-a-kind souvenirs and handcrafted things in the area's mix of conventional stores, artisan boutiques, and local markets. From Venetian masks and Murano glass to locally made wine and food, Cannaregio provides many chances to purchase unique goods that showcase the city's exquisite craftsmanship and culture. You can also experience the local way of life and meet Venetians as they go about their everyday lives in the neighborhood's markets, such the one at Campo dei Mori.

Even though Cannaregio offers a lot of benefits, there are a few things to think about before choosing to remain in this area. Its short distance from some of Venice's most well-known sites, such St. Mark's Square and the Doge's Palace, could be a disadvantage. Even though you may still walk to these sights, depending on where you are in Cannaregio, it might take you 20 to 30 minutes to get there. This distance, though, can also be considered a benefit since it lets you avoid the crowds and have a more tranquil and genuine Venice experience. If you would rather not walk, you can easily take the vaporetto to the city's major attractions thanks to the neighborhood's excellent transportation connections.

Another factor to take into account is that tourists seeking a vibrant and busy setting might not find Cannaregio's more sedate and residential ambiance appealing. Dorsoduro or San Marco would be better options if you want to be close to the action, with easy access to Venice's nightlife and cultural events. But Cannaregio is a great option for anyone who like genuineness, affordability, and a slower pace.

Staying in Cannaregio gives you the chance to see Venice from a local's point of view while also taking advantage of the neighborhood's cost and proximity. Its affordable lodging and dining options make it accessible to a diverse range of tourists, and its lively food scene, peaceful ambiance, and rich history make it an excellent starting point for exploring the city. Cannaregio offers the ideal mix of convenience and authenticity, enabling you to fully experience the beauty and culture of this remarkable place, whether you are traveling to

Venice for the first time or coming back to see a different aspect of the city. You may have a more personal and unforgettable trip to Venice while still being close to its most famous attractions if you choose Cannaregio as your starting point.

Dorsoduro

Since every region of Venice offers a different atmosphere and experience, choose the ideal district for your lodging is a crucial element of trip planning. Dorsoduro is a great option for tourists looking for a calmer, more laid-back setting with a strong artistic and cultural ambiance. One of Venice's most quaint and attractive neighborhoods is Dorsoduro, which is located on the southern side of the Grand Canal. It is a popular among artists, students, and those seeking a more sedate side of Venice because of its stunning canals, old buildings, and thriving arts sector. You may take in the beauty and culture of the city while staying in Dorsoduro, away from the thronging throngs that are frequently present in more central locations like San Marco. For those who wish to see Venice more slowly while yet being close to its great attractions, this neighborhood strikes the ideal balance between creativity and inspiration and peace and quiet.

With good cause, Dorsoduro is frequently referred to as Venice's artistic center. Some of the most significant art institutions in the city may be found in the district, such as the Peggy Guggenheim Collection, a modern art museum housed in a magnificent palazzo on the Grand Canal, and the Gallerie dell'Accademia, which has a world-class collection of

Venetian Renaissance art. Dorsoduro is a center of inspiration and creativity thanks to these cultural treasures, which draw art enthusiasts from all over the world. Apart from its museums, Dorsoduro is renowned for its numerous art galleries, workshops, and studios where you may find the creations of regional craftspeople. Small galleries and stores selling one-of-a-kind, handcrafted goods, such as jewelry, glassware, paintings, and sculptures, are frequently found throughout the neighborhood. You may explore Venice's vibrant contemporary art scene and become fully immersed in its artistic legacy by staying in Dorsoduro.

The tranquil and relaxed ambiance of Dorsoduro is one of the primary benefits of visiting. Dorsoduro is a great option for those who wish to avoid the hustle and bustle of the more tourist-heavy neighborhoods because it feels more residential and less crowded than the busy streets of San Marco or Cannaregio. The neighborhood's attractive squares, like Campo Santa Margherita and Campo San Barnaba, provide a laid-back atmosphere where you can sit and have a coffee or a glass of wine while taking in the scenery. Its peaceful lanes and canals are ideal for leisurely strolls. Dorsoduro is a terrific area to relax and see the more genuine aspect of Venice because of its slower pace and peaceful atmosphere.

Dorsoduro is nevertheless easily accessible and has good connections to the rest of Venice, despite its peaceful setting. Major sites including St. Mark's Square, the Rialto Bridge, and the islands of Giudecca and San Giorgio Maggiore are all within a short stroll or vaporetto ride from the district.

Connecting Dorsoduro to the San Marco district, the Accademia Bridge—one of just four bridges that span the Grand Canal—makes it simple to get to the city's most well-known sites while remaining in a more tranquil region. Zattere, Accademia, and Ca' Rezzonico are just a few of the vaporetto locations in Dorsoduro that offer easy access to various areas of the city and the nearby lagoon. Because of its accessibility and calm, Dorsoduro is a great starting point for visiting Venice.

Dorsoduro's thriving food and drink culture is another reason to visit. You may savor delectable regional cuisine in a laid-back and friendly atmosphere in the neighborhood's many restaurants, trattorias, and bacari (Venetian wine bars). Since many of these places are favored by locals rather than visitors, you may enjoy real Venetian cuisine away from the crowds. The bustling waterfront promenade along the Zattere, which offers a variety of eateries and cafés with breathtaking views of the Giudecca Canal, is what makes Dorsoduro so well-known. Both locals and tourists frequently congregate here to eat or drink while taking in the sunset over the sea. Dorsoduro offers a variety of dining options to fit every taste and price range, whether you're searching for a quick snack, a romantic supper, or a classic Venetian aperitivo.

Fresh produce, seafood, and other regional specialties may be found in Dorsoduro's many local markets and shops, in addition to its eateries and cafés. You can get supplies for a picnic or a lunch at your lodging and get a taste of Venetian daily life at the local markets. Shops and stores in Dorsoduro also sell a variety of handcrafted and distinctive goods, such as apparel, accessories, Venetian masks, and Murano glass. Compared to the busier parts of Venice, shopping in Dorsoduro is more laid-back and pleasurable, and it offers a chance to support regional companies and artists.

Dorsoduro provides a variety of lodging choices to accommodate a range of tastes and price ranges. A variety of boutique hotels, guesthouses, and vacation rentals can be found in the area; many of them are housed in ancient structures with stunning views of the lagoon or canals. Because many of the lodgings in Dorsoduro are smaller and family-run, offering a cozy and personalized touch, staying here enables you to get a more intimate and genuine experience of Venice. Dorsoduro offers a variety of lodging options, including comfortable apartments with a classic Venetian ambiance and opulent hotels with contemporary conveniences.

The chance to take part in local festivals and activities is one of the special features of visiting Dorsoduro. From processions and concerts to art exhibits and culinary festivals, Dorsoduro organizes a wide range of religious and cultural events all year long. These gatherings give visitors an opportunity to interact with the locals and get a taste of Venice's traditions and customs. Your journey can take on a unique and unforgettable dimension if you choose to stay in Dorsoduro during one of these events.

Even though Dorsoduro offers a lot of benefits, there are a few things to think about before choosing to remain in this area. Its short distance from some of Venice's most well-known sites, like the Doge's Palace and St. Mark's Basilica, could be a disadvantage. Even though you may still walk to these places, depending on where you are in Dorsoduro, it could take you 20 to 30 minutes. This distance, though, can also be considered a benefit since it lets you avoid the crowds and have a more tranquil and genuine Venice experience. If you would rather not walk, you can easily take the vaporetto to the city's major attractions thanks to the neighborhood's excellent transportation connections.

Another factor to take into account is that tourists seeking a vibrant and busy setting might not find Dorsoduro's more sedate and residential ambiance appealing. Perhaps San Marco or Cannaregio are better options if you want to be right in the middle of things, with easy access to Venice's nightlife and cultural events. However, Dorsoduro is a great option for anyone who appreciate peace, creativity, and a slower pace.

A rare chance to see Venice from a different angle—one that is more serene, creative, and genuine—is provided by staying in Dorsoduro. Its superb dining, shopping, and lodging options guarantee a pleasant and enjoyable stay, and its lively arts scene, rich cultural legacy, and serene atmosphere make it an ideal starting point for exploring the city. Dorsoduro offers the ideal fusion of beauty, culture, and peace, enabling you to fully experience Venice's allure while having a more personal and unforgettable experience, whether you are traveling there for the first time or coming back to see a different aspect of the city. By making Dorsoduro your starting point, you may take your time exploring the city and make enduring memories of your visit to this unique location.

Santa Croce, San Polo, and Castello

Since every neighborhood in Venice offers a different experience and environment, choose the ideal location for your lodging is an important aspect of trip preparation. Despite being some of the most quaint and genuine parts of the city, the neighborhoods of Castello, San Polo, and Santa Croce are sometimes disregarded by tourists, who are drawn to the popular places like San Marco or Dorsoduro. These neighborhoods are undiscovered treasures that offer a more sedate and authentic Venice experience, away from the bustling tourist centers. They are perfect for tourists who wish to learn more about the city's fascinating past, take in its splendor more slowly, and find areas of Venice that don't seem to have been overrun by tourists. You may see a distinct side of Venice by staying in one of these areas; it's more tranquil, genuine, and closely tied to the city's customs and everyday life.

The largest of Venice's six districts, Castello spans from the busy neighborhoods around St. Mark's Square to the more sedate, residential regions of the city. It is a neighborhood of contrasts, having both peaceful nooks where residents go about their everyday lives and bustling avenues brimming with eateries and businesses. The Arsenale, a historic shipyard that once served as the center of Venice's naval might, is one of

Castello's highlights. In addition to being an interesting place to visit today, the Arsenale hosts cultural events like the Venice Biennale, which is one of the most prominent art exhibitions in the world. Staying in Castello allows you to take in this special fusion of culture and history in a more laid-back and genuine setting.

For tourists who wish to get away from the crowds and experience the local way of life, the eastern region of Castello, also referred to as the "true Castello," is very alluring. Narrow streets, peaceful squares, and tiny canals define this neighborhood, where you may observe kids playing, neighbors conversing, and clothes hanging from windows. Major landmarks like the Doge's Palace and St. Mark's Basilica are still easily accessible on foot, but it feels like a world away from the crowded tourist regions. The area is also home to a number of exquisite churches, including San Francesco della Vigna, renowned for its serene cloisters and magnificent architecture, and San Pietro di Castello, the first cathedral of Venice. For those who wish to see the real Venice, Castello is a great spot to stay because of its charming neighborhood markets, traditional bakeries, and family-run trattorias.

Despite being one of Venice's smallest neighborhoods, San Polo is teeming with charm and history. San Polo, which is on the western bank of the Grand Canal, is most famous for the colorful and lively Rialto Market, which has long been a center of Venetian life. With its extensive selection of fresh vegetables, seafood, and regional specialties, the market is a must-visit for foodies. You may tour this bustling market and take advantage of the great local cuisine, which includes classic osterias, wine bars, and cafés, if you choose to stay in San Polo. One of Venice's most famous monuments, the Rialto Bridge, is surrounded by a flurry of activity, but as you get farther away from the bridge, you'll find more peaceful streets and secret squares where you can get away from the people and enjoy the neighborhood's charm.

Some of Venice's most exquisite churches and historical landmarks may be found in San Polo. Titian and other famous artists' works can be found at the beautiful Gothic church known as the Basilica di Santa Maria Gloriosa dei Frari, or simply the Frari. The Scuola Grande di San Rocco is a stunning structure nearby that is embellished with stunning pieces by Tintoretto. San Polo is a fantastic option for art and history lovers who wish to remain in a beautiful and historically significant area because of these cultural gems. San Polo is a fantastic choice for tourists who wish to be near the major sights but still have a more sedate and genuine experience because, despite its central location, it feels more local and intimate than some of the other districts.

Another undiscovered treasure that provides a distinctive and serene ambiance is Santa Croce, the smallest and least visited neighborhood in Venice. Santa Croce, which is just west of San Polo, is frequently disregarded by tourists but offers plenty to those who take the time to explore. In addition to its combination of old structures and contemporary conveniences, the neighborhood is renowned for its serene streets, quaint squares, and lovely canals. Being adjacent to Piazzale Roma, the city's main bus terminal, and the Santa Lucia rail station makes Santa Croce one of the most convenient places to stay in Venice. Because of this, it is the perfect option for tourists who wish to have convenient access to transit while yet being able to stroll to the main sights of Venice.

The Natural History Museum of Venice is housed in the old Fondaco dei Turchi, one of Santa Croce's main attractions. Families with children will especially love this museum, which is a terrific place to learn about the city's natural and cultural past. Numerous exquisite churches, including San Giacomo dell'Orio, which is renowned for its distinctive architecture and serene interior, can be found in Santa Croce. Away from the crowds and bustle of the more touristic neighborhoods, the neighborhood's peaceful alleyways and secret spots make it an excellent place to stroll and explore Venice's lesser-known side.

Apart from its historical and cultural landmarks, Santa Croce provides a range of retail and dining opportunities for both locals and tourists. The neighborhood's stores and marketplaces offer a blend of traditional and modern goods, and its restaurants and trattorias serve outstanding Venetian food at more reasonable costs than those in the more central areas. Santa Croce is an excellent area to experience Venetian daily life and have a more real and affordable stay in the city because to its laid-back and unpretentious ambiance.

Although each of Castello, San Polo, and Santa Croce has its own distinct personality and allure, they are all distinguished from Venice's more tourist-heavy neighborhoods by their sense of genuineness and peace. These communities provide an opportunity to get a closer, more personal look into the city's rich history, culture, and everyday life. Staying in one of these undiscovered jewels will offer you a fascinating and fulfilling experience that lets you see a distinct side of Venice, regardless of whether you are drawn to the tranquil beauty of Santa Croce, the lively energy of San Polo, or the ancient charm of Castello. You may get the best of both worlds by booking your lodging in one of these neighborhoods: quick access to the city's top attractions and a tranquil haven where you can unwind and take in Venice's allure.

Accommodation Types

Luxurious Hotels

One of the greatest ways to completely experience the beauty and charm of Venice, one of the most captivating towns on earth, is to stay in a posh hotel with a view of the canal. The city's canals are its lifeblood, and nothing quite sums up the allure of Venice like waking up to the sight of gondolas sailing by your window or the glistening reflections of old buildings on the water. Venice provides a selection of upscale hotels for tourists looking for an opulent stay, combining breathtaking canal views with top-notch facilities, first-rate service, and a dash of Venetian flair. For those who wish to enjoy the best lodging Venice has to offer, these hotels, which are located in some of the most famous and charming areas of the city, offer an experience that will never be forgotten. The top five luxury hotels in Venice with views of the canal are included below, along with information on their locations, amenities, pricing ranges, and how to get there from the main airports. You will also get details on how to reserve these hotels in order to guarantee a smooth and delightful visit.

The Aman Venice, one of Venice's most famous luxury hotels, is located along the Grand Canal in the San Polo neighborhood. Located in a 16th-century palazzo, this hotel is renowned for its lavish interiors, which include elaborate chandeliers, gilded ceilings, and original murals. Many of the rooms and suites at the Aman Venice enjoy stunning views of the Grand Canal and are roomy and tastefully decorated. A fine-dining restaurant with international and Venetian fare, a spa, a private garden, and individualized concierge services are among the hotel's features. Depending on the time of year and the type of room, rates at the Aman Venice normally start at about €1,500 per night. The most practical and opulent way to get to the Aman Venice from Marco Polo Airport is to take a private water taxi straight to the hotel's own dock. As an alternative, you can walk a short distance to the hotel after taking the Alilaguna water bus to the Rialto stop. You can make reservations at the Aman Venice via the hotel's main website, upscale travel companies, or internet booking services like Booking.com or Expedia.

The Gritti Palace, a Luxury Collection Hotel in the San Marco neighborhood, is another outstanding choice for opulent lodging with views of the canal. Located right on the Grand Canal, this ancient hotel provides breathtaking views of famous sites including the Santa Maria della Salute Basilica. With rooms and suites that include antique furniture, chandeliers made of Murano glass, and opulent textiles, the Gritti Palace is renowned for its classic elegance. A gourmet restaurant, a rooftop patio, a spa, and a private boat for excursions are among the hotel's features. The Gritti Palace is a popular option for tourists looking for an incredibly opulent experience because its rates start at about €1,200 per night. You can take a private water taxi straight to the hotel's dock from Marco Polo Airport or take the Alilaguna water bus to the Santa Maria del Giglio stop, which is a short stroll from the hotel, to get to the Gritti Palace. The hotel's own website, Marriott Bonvoy (because it is a member of the Luxury Collection), or reliable travel websites can all be used to make reservations.

A great option for guests seeking a contemporary luxury experience with views of the canal is the JW Marriott Venice Resort & Spa. This hotel offers a distinctive and peaceful setting away from the bustle of the city center, located on Isola delle Rose, a private island in the Venetian Lagoon. Some of the elegantly designed modern rooms and suites at the JW Marriott provide views of the lagoon and the skyline of Venice. The hotel has a spa, a rooftop pool, several restaurants, and beautiful gardens. The JW Marriott Venice is a more cost-effective choice than some of the other upscale hotels in Venice, with rates starting at about €600 per night. You can take a private water taxi straight from Marco Polo Airport to the JW Marriott, or you can take the Alilaguna water bus to San Marco and then board the hotel's free shuttle boat. Reservations can be made via online travel agencies, Marriott Bonvoy, or the hotel's official website.

Another famous luxury hotel in Venice is the Hotel Danieli, a Luxury Collection hotel, which is located in the Castello neighborhood close to St. Mark's Square. Located in a former palace, this ancient hotel is renowned for its opulent interiors, which feature marble stairs, elaborate ceilings, and antique furnishings. Beautiful views of the Grand Canal or the Venetian Lagoon can be seen from many of the Hotel Danieli's rooms and suites. Personalized concierge services, a bar, and a restaurant with panoramic views are among the hotel's attractions. Depending on the season and kind of hotel, rates at the Hotel Danieli start at about €1,000 per night. You may either take a private water taxi straight to the hotel's dock from Marco Polo Airport or take the Alilaguna water bus to the San Zaccaria stop, which is only a short stroll from the hotel. Reservations can be made via Marriott Bonvoy, the hotel's official website, or reliable travel agencies.

Lastly, the Ca' Sagredo Hotel is a boutique luxury hotel located right on the Grand Canal in the Cannaregio neighborhood. This 15th-century palazzo has undergone exquisite restoration to become a five-star hotel that blends contemporary luxury with historic charm. Many of the sophisticated rooms and suites of the Ca' Sagredo Hotel have breathtaking views of the Grand Canal. The hotel has a fitness facility, a rooftop patio, and a fine-dining restaurant. The Ca' Sagredo Hotel is a more affordable choice for tourists looking for opulent lodging with canal views, with rates starting at about €700 per night. You may either take a private water taxi straight from Marco Polo Airport to the Ca' Sagredo Hotel or take the Alilaguna water bus to the Ca' d'Oro stop, which is a short stroll from the hotel. Online booking platforms, premium travel agents, and the hotel's official website are all options for making reservations. It's crucial to make reservations in advance for a luxury hotel in Venice because these establishments are highly sought after, particularly during the busiest tourist times. The hotel's official website allows you to make direct reservations and frequently has the best prices and special packages. As an alternative, you can utilize online travel companies like Booking.com, Expedia, or Hotels.com, which let you read reviews from previous customers and compare pricing. Working with a luxury travel agency or concierge service can help you book the best rooms and offer extra services like private excursions and airport transfers for a more customized experience. Regardless of the approach you take, it is advised to make reservations in advance to guarantee availability and the best prices.

A memorable experience that lets you completely appreciate Venice's beauty and charm is staying in a luxury hotel with a view of the canal. You will undoubtedly have a wonderful and distinctively Venetian stay whether you opt for the Aman Venice's extravagance, the Gritti Palace's historic elegance, the JW Marriott's contemporary luxury, the Hotel Danieli's legendary grandeur, or the Ca' Sagredo Hotel's boutique charm. Finding the ideal lodging to make your trip to Venice genuinely remarkable requires careful consideration of your tastes, financial situation, and itinerary.

Charming B&Bs and Boutique Hotels

Many tourists find that the best way to enjoy Venice's distinct ambiance is to stay in a boutique hotel or a quaint bed & breakfast. Venice is a city that radiates romance and charm. When compared to larger hotels, these more intimate, smaller lodgings frequently offer a more genuine and intimate experience, making you feel more a part of the city and its customs. In Venice, boutique hotels and bed and breakfasts frequently occupy ancient structures, such as palazzos that date back centuries or former merchant residences, and blend contemporary conveniences with classic Venetian design. Many of these lodgings are family-owned and provide individualized attention and friendly hospitality to make your stay unforgettable. Boutique hotels and bed and breakfasts are great options for tourists that appreciate personality, fine details, and a more laid-back setting. The top five boutique hotels and quaint bed and breakfasts in Venice are included here, along with information on their locations, amenities, pricing range, and how to get there from the main airports in the city. To guarantee a seamless and pleasurable experience, you will also find information on how to reserve these accommodations.

The San Marco neighborhood's Corte di Gabriela is one of Venice's most renowned boutique hotels. This sophisticated hotel offers the ideal fusion of contemporary style and classic Venetian charm, all housed in a beautifully renovated 19th-century edifice. At Corte di Gabriela, each room and suite is uniquely furnished with opulent furnishings, environmentally sustainable materials, and considerate embellishments like handcrafted Murano glass. The hotel offers a delicious breakfast prepared with products that are sourced locally, a library, and a peaceful courtyard area. The average nightly rate at Corte di Gabriela is between €300 and €500, depending on the time of year and kind of lodging. You may either take a private water taxi straight to the Sant'Angelo vaporetto stop from Marco Polo Airport or take the Alilaguna water bus to the same point and walk a short distance to the hotel. You can make a reservation via the hotel's official website, where you could find special deals, or through reliable online booking services like Booking.com or Expedia.

The Ca' Pisani Hotel, which is close to the Gallerie dell'Accademia in the Dorsoduro neighborhood, is another great choice for boutique lodging. Located in a 14th-century building, this chic hotel is renowned for its Art Deco-inspired décor that provide a distinctive and elegant ambiance. Ca' Pisani offers large rooms with contemporary conveniences including air conditioning, flat-screen TVs, and opulent bathrooms. The hotel also has a restaurant that serves Mediterranean and Venetian food, a modest health area with a steam bath, and a rooftop terrace with panoramic views. The Ca' Pisani Hotel is a fantastic option for tourists looking for a boutique experience with a dash of luxury, with rates ranging from €250 to €400 per night. You can take a private water taxi to the Accademia vaporetto stop from Marco Polo Airport, or you can take the Alilaguna water bus to Zattere and walk a short distance to the hotel. Online travel agents or the hotel's website are the two options for making reservations.

Cima Rosa is a great option for those who want the warm and welcoming ambiance of a bed and breakfast. With breathtaking views of the water, this quaint B&B is located right on the Grand Canal in the Santa Croce neighborhood. The antique palace where Cima Rosa is located has only a few exquisitely decorated rooms, each with a distinct personality. High ceilings, huge windows that bring in lots of natural light, and antique furnishings are all features of the soft, elegantly furnished rooms. Among the B&B's features are a delectable prepared breakfast, a tranquil garden, and attentive service from the kind hosts. Depending on the accommodation and season, Cima Rosa rates vary from €200 to €400 per night. You may take a private water taxi straight to the hotel's dock from Marco Polo Airport or take the Alilaguna water bus to the San Stae stop, which is only a short stroll away, to get to Cima Rosa. Reservations can be made using Booking.com or Airbnb, or via the B&B's official website.

Locanda Vivaldi, a boutique hotel close to St. Mark's Square in the Castello neighborhood, is another noteworthy choice. This little hotel is located in a building with a long history and is named after the well-known musician Antonio Vivaldi. With elaborate furnishings, chandeliers made of Murano glass, and sumptuous textiles, the apartments of Locanda Vivaldi are furnished in the traditional Venetian style. The hotel features a rooftop terrace with stunning city views, and many of the rooms have views of the Venetian Lagoon. A restaurant, a bar, and a private water taxi dock are among the facilities. The cost per night at Locanda Vivaldi varies based on the season and style of room, from €250 to €500. You may either take a private water taxi straight to the hotel's dock from Marco Polo Airport or take the Alilaguna water bus to the San Zaccaria stop, which is only a short stroll from the hotel. Reservations can be made via online travel companies and the hotel's official website.

Lastly, a little stroll from the Accademia Bridge in the San Marco neighborhood lies the Novecento Boutique Hotel, a hidden gem. The unique decor of this family-run hotel, which blends Venetian, Mediterranean, and Oriental influences, is well-known for its friendly hospitality. Novecento offers comfortable and elegant rooms with handmade textiles, antique furniture, and contemporary conveniences like free Wi-Fi and air conditioning. A library, a tranquil courtyard garden, and a delectable breakfast prepared with organic and regional products are among the hotel's features. The Novecento Boutique Hotel charges between €200 and €400 a night, depending on the time of year and type of room. You may either take a private water taxi to the Sant'Angelo vaporetto stop from Marco Polo Airport or take the Alilaguna water bus to the same stop and walk a short distance to the hotel. Reservations can be made directly on the hotel's website or via websites such as Booking.com or Expedia.

It's crucial to make reservations in advance for a boutique hotel or bed and breakfast in Venice because these smaller lodging options frequently have limited availability, particularly during the busiest travel seasons. The best alternative is frequently to book directly through the hotel's own website, as it may offer special packages or bargains. Another option is to utilize internet travel companies like Booking.com, Expedia, or Hotels.com, which let you check availability, read reviews, and compare prices. Consider using a travel agency or concierge service for a more individualized experience. They can assist you in finding the ideal lodging and offer extra services like private tours and airport transfers. Regardless of the approach you take, it is advised to make your reservation as soon as possible to guarantee your desired dates and type of accommodation.

One of the best ways to enjoy Venice's distinct character and hospitality is to stay in a boutique hotel or quaint B&B. You will undoubtedly have a comfortable and unforgettable stay whether you decide on the elegance of Corte di Gabriela, the Art Deco style of Ca' Pisani, the quaint appeal of Cima Rosa, the historic beauty of Locanda Vivaldi, or the eclectic ambiance of Novecento Boutique Hotel. Finding the ideal lodging to make your trip to Venice genuinely unforgettable requires careful consideration of your tastes, financial situation, and itinerary.

Low-Cost Apartments and Hostels

It can be difficult to find inexpensive lodging in Venice because of the city's well-known tourist attractions and exorbitant costs. On the other hand, hostels and apartments are great choices for tourists who are concerned about their spending limits. In addition to saving you money, these kinds of lodgings provide special chances to see Venice in a more practical and intimate manner. While flats are great for families, parties, or anyone who appreciates privacy and the ease of having their own space, hostels are best for backpackers, single people, or people who like to meet other travelers. Both choices let you see Venice without sacrificing comfort or location, and many of them are in quaint areas with quick access to the city's top attractions. The top five inexpensive hostels and apartments in Venice are listed here, along with information on their locations, amenities, price ranges, and how to get there from the main airports in the city. To guarantee a seamless and pleasurable stay, you will also find information on how to reserve these rooms.

Generator Venice, which is located on the island of Giudecca, is one of the most well-liked inexpensive hostels in Venice. This chic and contemporary hostel is ideal for both single people and small groups because it provides a variety of lodging choices, such as private rooms and dorm beds. The hostel has a large common space, a bar, and a café where visitors can unwind and mingle. It is set in a tastefully renovated, modern building. A 24-hour reception desk, lockers, and free Wi-Fi are among the facilities. Depending on the season, rates at Generator Venice range from about €30 per night for a dorm bed to €100 per night for a private room. You can take the Alilaguna water bus to the Zitelle stop, which is only a short stroll from the hostel, to get there from Marco Polo Airport. In addition to websites like Hostelworld and Booking.com, reservations can be made via the hostel's official website.

A&O Venice Mestre, located in the village of Mestre on the mainland, is another great choice for tourists on a tight budget. Even though it's not on one of Venice's main islands, this hostel is a fantastic option for budget travelers who still want convenient access to the city. In addition to individual rooms and dorm beds, A&O Venice Mestre has contemporary amenities like a communal kitchen, a lounge area, and a bar. Due to the hostel's handy location next to the Mestre train station, it takes only ten minutes to travel by bus or train to Venice's historic center. Dormitory beds at A&O Venice Mestre start at about €20 per night, while private rooms cost €60 per night. You may walk a short distance to the hostel from Marco Polo Airport after taking a bus or taxi to Mestre train station. Reservations can be made via Hostelworld, the hostel's official website, or other online travel agencies.

The Venice Apartments San Marco is an excellent option for those who value the seclusion and practicality of an apartment. Located in the center of Venice, a short stroll from St. Mark's Square, these self-catering flats provide a cozy and reasonably priced substitute for conventional hotels. The apartments come completely equipped with free Wi-Fi, air conditioning, and a kitchenette. Families or parties who wish to cook for themselves and have more room to unwind will find them perfect. Depending on the size of the apartment and the time of year, rates for Venice Apartments San Marco start at about €100 per night. From Marco Polo Airport, you may either take a private water taxi straight to the San Marco neighborhood or take the Alilaguna water bus to the San Zaccaria stop and then walk a short distance to the flats. Platforms like as Airbnb,

Booking.com, or the official website of the property can be used to make reservations.

Ca' della Scimmia, which is close to the Rialto Bridge in the San Polo neighborhood, is another excellent apartment choice. With a hint of Venetian elegance, this boutique apartment complex offers chic, contemporary lodging. With a living area, a kitchenette, and a private toilet, each apartment is a convenient and comfortable option for tourists. With quick access to the Grand Canal, the Rialto Market, and other important sites, the location is superb. Depending on the size of the apartment and the time of year, rates at Ca' della Scimmia start at about €120 per night. From Marco Polo Airport, you may either take a private water taxi to the Rialto neighborhood or take the Alilaguna water bus to the Rialto stop and then walk a short distance to the flats. Reservations can be made via Airbnb, the official property website, or other online booking services.

Ostello Santa Fosca is an inexpensive hostel in the Cannaregio neighborhood for travelers who prefer a more authentic Venetian experience. Located in a historic structure, this quaint hostel provides reasonably priced private rooms and bunk beds. The hostel is an excellent option for tourists on a tight budget who want a quiet and comfortable place to stay because it has a calm garden, a communal kitchen, and free Wi-Fi. Dormitory beds at Ostello Santa Fosca start at about €25 per night, while private rooms cost about €70 per night. From Marco Polo Airport, you may walk a short distance to the hostel after taking the Alilaguna water bus to the Ca' d'Oro stop. Reservations can be made via the main hostel website, Booking.com, or Hostelworld.

Budget hostels and apartments in Venice are frequently in high demand, particularly during the busiest tourism seasons, so it's best to book in advance. The best option is frequently to make a direct reservation via the property's own website, as this may provide special offers or discounts. As an alternative, you can research costs, read reviews, and verify availability by using online travel agencies like Hostelworld, Booking.com, or Airbnb. Hostelworld is a very helpful website for hostels because it focuses on low-cost lodging and offers comprehensive details about each establishment. Both Booking.com and Airbnb are great options for flats because they provide a large selection and let you narrow down your search according to your tastes and price range.

A convenient and reasonably priced method to take in Venice's beauty and charm without going over budget is to stay in a hostel or apartment. You are sure to find a choice that fits your needs and budget, whether you choose with the chic Generator Venice, the practical A&O Venice Mestre, the conveniently placed Venice Apartments San Marco, the contemporary Ca' della Scimmia, or the classic Ostello Santa Fosca. Finding the ideal lodging to make your trip to Venice memorable and pleasurable requires careful consideration of your tastes, travel schedule, and financial constraints.

Tips for Booking

Since Venice is one of the world's most visited tourist sites, booking lodging there demands great thought and preparation. Finding the ideal spot to stay at the best price might be difficult due to the city's distinctive layout, strong demand for lodging, and abundance of possibilities. But with the correct strategy, you may find a cozy and practical place to stay that suits your tastes and price range. Whether you're searching for a self-catering apartment, a luxury hotel, a boutique bed and breakfast, or an affordable hostel, there are a few ways to acquire the best rates and make sure the booking process goes well. Before making your ultimate choice, it's also critical to take into account elements like location, amenities, and available transit. A thorough breakdown of how to locate the finest lodging offers in Venice, things to think about before making a reservation, and examples of five distinct kinds of accommodations—along with information on their features, pricing ranges, and accessibility from the main airports—are provided below.

Making reservations as soon as possible is one of the most crucial pieces of advice for locating the greatest lodging offers in Venice. Due to its small size and popularity, hotels, hostels, and apartments in Venice tend to fill up rapidly, particularly during the busiest tourism seasons (spring and summer) and during significant events like the Biennale or the Venice Carnival. In addition to offering you more alternatives, making reservations several months in advance enables you to benefit from early-bird discounts and reduced rates. You can change or cancel your reservation without losing money because many hotels and booking websites have lenient cancellation policies. For instance, a high-end hotel such as the Hotel Danieli, which is close to St. Mark's Square, frequently provides early booking savings for its exquisite rooms and suites, which cost between €1,000 and €2,500 a night. The hotel has a private dock for water taxis, views of the lagoon, and a restaurant on the rooftop. You can take a private water taxi straight from Marco Polo Airport to the Hotel Danieli, or you can take the Alilaguna water bus to the San Zaccaria stop, which is a short stroll away. Reservations can be made using reliable travel websites like Booking.com or the hotel's official website, Marriott Bonvoy.

Comparing costs across other booking platforms is another important tactic for locating the greatest offers. You can look for lodging on websites like Booking.com, Expedia, Hotels.com, and Agoda by selecting your interests, vacation dates, and budget. You may make an informed choice by using the customer reviews and ratings that are frequently included on these platforms. Furthermore, some sites provide discounts or loyalty programs to loyal users, which might help you save money on your reservation. For instance, the San Marco district's Corte di Gabriela is a fantastic choice if you're searching for a boutique hotel. Depending on the time of year, the opulent rooms at this environmentally conscious hotel cost between €300 and €500 a night. A gourmet breakfast, a library, and a courtyard garden are among the facilities. You may either take a private water taxi to the neighboring Sant'Angelo vaporetto stop or take the Alilaguna water bus to the same stop and walk a short distance to get to Corte di Gabriela from Marco Polo Airport. Reservations can be made via the hotel's website or online travel agencies such as Booking.com or Expedia.

Finding better rates on lodging in Venice might also be facilitated by being flexible with your visit dates. Weekends, holidays, and the busiest travel seasons typically have higher rates for hotels and other places to stay. Consider traveling to Venice in the off-season, which usually lasts from November to February (not including the Carnival season), if your schedule permits. You can frequently find cheaper rates and take advantage of the city's calmer, more laid-back ambiance during this time. For instance, those on a tight budget can think about booking a room at Generator Venice, a chic hostel on the island of Giudecca. Dormitory beds start at about €30 per night, while private rooms cost about €100 per night. The hostel has a large common space, a café, and a bar. You can take the Alilaguna water bus from Marco Polo Airport to the Zitelle stop, which is a short stroll from the hostel, to get to Generator Venice. Reservations can be made using Booking.com, Hostelworld, or the hostel's website.

It is crucial to think about the location and how it fits into your trip schedule when making reservations for lodging in Venice. Each of Venice's six major districts has its own distinct personality and points of interest. Although the San Marco district is the busiest and most costly, staying there puts you close to important sights like the Doge's Palace and St. Mark's Basilica. However, areas like Castello, Dorsoduro, and

Cannaregio provide a more genuine and local experience, frequently at a lower cost. For instance, the San Polo district's Ca' della Scimmia boutique apartment complex provides chic and contemporary lodging with nightly rates starting at about €120. Each apartment is a terrific option for families or groups because it has a kitchenette, a living space, and a private bathroom. You can take a private water taxi from Marco Polo Airport to the neighboring Rialto neighborhood or take the Alilaguna water bus to the Rialto stop and walk a short distance to get to Ca' della Scimmia. Booking.com, Airbnb, or the official website of the property can all be used to make reservations.

The facilities and services provided by the lodging are an additional crucial consideration when making a reservation. Features like free Wi-Fi, air conditioning, breakfast, or a 24-hour reception desk can be things you want to search for, depending on your needs and tastes. It is worthwhile to confirm whether the hotel can meet your food needs if you have special dietary requirements or are traveling with children. For instance, Venice Apartments San Marco is a sensible option for families or extended visits since it provides self-catering apartments with kitchenettes, air conditioning, and free Wi-Fi. Depending on the season and unit size, rates start at about €100 per night. You may either take a private water taxi to the San Marco district from Marco Polo Airport or take the Alilaguna water bus to the San Zaccaria stop and walk a short distance to get to Venice Apartments San Marco. Booking.com, Airbnb, or the official website of the property can all be used to make reservations.

Lastly, before confirming your reservation, it is crucial to research reviews and review the cancellation policy. Reviews from previous visitors can offer important information on the standard of the lodging, the staff's friendliness, and the entire experience. Recent reviews are more likely to represent the property's current condition, so pay attention to them. Additionally, pay close attention to the cancellation policy, particularly if your trip schedule is subject to change. When you book in advance, you can feel more at ease knowing that many lodgings provide free cancellation up until a specific date.

CHAPTER 4

THE FAMOUS ATTRACTIONS IN VENICE

Significant Landmarks

Piazza San Marco and St. Mark's Basilica

Two of Venice's most recognizable and important landmarks are St. Mark's Basilica and Piazza San Marco, which are must-see sights for any traveler. In addition to being architectural wonders, these sites in the center of Venice are also extremely significant historically, culturally, and religiously. Together, they attract millions of tourists annually and serve as the focal point of Venetian history and life. St. Mark's Basilica is one of the most well-known cathedrals in the world because of its magnificent Byzantine architecture, elaborate mosaics, and lengthy history. The majestic and graceful Piazza San Marco, sometimes known as "the drawing room of Europe," is encircled by old buildings and provides a lively environment along with stunning vistas. There are plenty of things to see and do to make your time at these locations genuinely remarkable, and visiting them is an experience that will never be forgotten.

In the center of Venice, on the eastern side of Piazza San Marco, is St. Mark's Basilica, also known as Basilica di San Marco. There are multiple routes to get there, and it is conveniently accessible from many locations throughout the city. You may take a vaporetto, or water bus, from the Santa Lucia train station to the San Marco stop, which is only a short stroll from the basilica, if you are traveling to Venice by train. You may take in views of the city's historic structures and the Grand Canal while traveling by vaporetto, which is both convenient and picturesque. If you are coming from Marco Polo Airport, you can book a private water taxi for a quicker and more direct ride, or you can take the Alilaguna water bus to the San Marco stop. Most neighborhoods in Venice are accessible by foot from St. Mark's Basilica, and the stroll itself is delightful as you wind through the city's quaint alleyways and canals.

Famous for its exquisite design and minute details, St. Mark's Basilica is a masterpiece of Byzantine architecture. The relics of St. Mark the Evangelist were transported from Alexandria to Venice and placed in the basilica when it was first constructed in the ninth century. Venice's position as a strong maritime republic is reflected in the church's expansion and international treasures over the ages. The basilica's façade, which is embellished with intricate mosaics, sculptures, and carvings, is among its most remarkable characteristics. The renowned bronze horses of St. Mark, which were transported to Venice from Constantinople in the thirteenth century, are displayed above the five arched doorways, which are embellished with elaborate decorations.

A stunning display of mosaics covering the basilica's walls, ceilings, and domes welcomes guests within. These mosaics, which are composed of small pieces of gold leaf and colored glass, show events from St. Mark's life and the Bible. One of the basilica's most striking characteristics are the glistening gold mosaics, which inspire awe and astonishment. Another focal point of the interior is the Pala d'Oro, a stunning altarpiece encrusted with precious stones and crafted from gold. Visitors must view this magnificent example of medieval craftsmanship, which is located behind the main altar.

Climbing to the Loggia dei Cavalli, the balcony above the main door, is one of the greatest ways to get the most of your visit to St. Mark's Basilica. You may take in breathtaking views of Piazza San Marco and the surroundings from here. The balcony also offers a closer view of the basilica's façade's fine features and the bronze horses. The Treasury, which contains a collection of priceless relics like as reliquaries, chalices, and other sacred objects, is another distinctive aspect of the basilica. Venice's rich history and cultural ties are reflected in these treasures, which were gathered over many centuries.

The biggest and most well-known square in Venice is Piazza San Marco, which is located right outside the basilica. The Doge's Palace, the Campanile (bell tower), and the Procuratie—once the headquarters of Venetian officials—are among the historic structures that encircle it. With its many cafés, stores, and street entertainers, the square is a bustling, energetic area. Sitting at one of the outdoor cafés, like Caffè Florian or Gran Caffè Quadri, and enjoying a coffee or a glass of wine while soaking up the atmosphere is one of the most well-liked pastimes in Piazza San Marco. The square's appeal is largely attributed to these ancient cafés, which have been welcoming guests for generations.

Another must-see landmark in Piazza San Marco is the Campanile, also known as the bell tower. It provides sweeping views of Venice and the surrounding lagoon from its approximately 100-meter height. Upon ascending the tower via elevator, visitors can take in breath-taking views over the city's roofs, canals, and islands. Because it offers a distinctive viewpoint of Venice's famous sites, the Campanile is also a fantastic location for photography.

Think about going on a guided tour to enhance your experience at St. Mark's Basilica and Piazza San Marco. Numerous tour operators provide guided tours that cover the history, architecture, and artwork of these sites in great detail. The history and culture of Piazza San Marco, as well as the value of the mosaics, sculptures, and other basilica features, may all be better understood with the aid of a guided tour. Additionally, some excursions provide skip-the-line access, which can help you save time when things become busy.

It is crucial to be aware that some portions of St. Mark's Basilica, like the Treasury, the Pala d'Oro, and the Loggia dei Cavalli, need an admission ticket if you intend to visit. Although general entrance to the basilica is free, there could be large lineups during the busiest travel seasons. You can reserve a timed entry ticket online at St. Mark's Basilica's official website (https://www.basilicasanmarco.it) to avoid standing in line. To assist you in planning your visit, the website also offers details about special events, opening hours, and other information. You can reach the basilica at +39 041 2708311 with any questions.

There is no admission charge for Piazza San Marco, which is accessible to everyone. There are separate tickets for the Doge's Palace and the Campanile, though, if you would like to visit them. While Doge's Palace tickets can be reserved via the official website (https://palazzoducale.visitmuve.it), Campanile tickets can be bought online or on-site. It is advised to make reservations in advance, particularly during peak times.

Doge's Palace with the Sighing Bridge

Two of Venice's most recognizable and important historical sites are the Doge's Palace and the Bridge of Sighs, which are must-sees for anybody traveling through this charming city. These two locations provide tourists with an insight into the magnificence and intricacy of the Venetian Republic and are intricately linked to the city's politics, history, and culture. For centuries, the Doge's Palace, also known as Palazzo Ducale, was the seat of government, the home of the Doge, Venice's chosen ruler, and the site of the city's courts and jails. A representation of Venice's judicial system, the Bridge of Sighs, which links the palace and the prison, is now one of the city's most photographed sites. When taken as a whole, these sites offer an enthralling voyage through Venice's history, and a visit is one to remember.

The Doge's Palace is located close to St. Mark's Basilica on the eastern side of Piazza San Marco in the center of Venice. It is conveniently accessible from all areas of the city due to its central placement. You may take a vaporetto, or water bus, from the Santa Lucia train station to the San Marco stop, which is only a short stroll from the palace, if you are traveling to Venice by train. You may take in views of the city's historic structures and the Grand Canal while traveling by vaporetto, which is both convenient and picturesque. If you are coming from Marco Polo Airport, you can book a private water taxi for a quicker and more direct ride, or you can take the Alilaguna water bus to the San Marco stop. The Doge's Palace is easily accessible by foot from the majority of areas for visitors staying in Venice, and the stroll itself is delightful as you wind through the city's quaint alleyways and canals.

Famous for its exquisite design and minute details, the Doge's Palace is a masterpiece of Gothic architecture. The palace's facade exudes grandeur and elegance because to its beautiful brickwork, pink-and-white marble façade, and elegant arches. The Porta della Carta, the elaborate entrance of the palace, is seen as you get closer. It is embellished with elaborate sculptures and carvings. This gate leads to the courtyard, where you may take in the stunning architecture of the palace as well as the Scala dei Giganti, a stately stairway with statues of Neptune and Mars on either side.

Visitors can tour a number of lavish chambers and halls within the Doge's Palace that were formerly utilized for ceremonial occasions, government meetings, and the administration of justice. The Hall of the Great Council, also known as the Sala del Maggior Consiglio, is one of the palace's main attractions and one of the biggest spaces in Europe. This spectacular hall boasts a breathtaking ceiling with gilded frames and intricate motifs, as well as rich frescoes and paintings by well-known artists like Tintoretto and Veronese. The Great Council, the Venetian Republic's ruling body, met in the hall, which is evidence of Venice's richness and influence during its heyday. The Sala del Collegio, also known as the Hall of the College, is another must-see space in the Doge's Palace. It was used as a gathering place for the Doge and his counselors. This room is renowned for its opulent décor, which includes paintings of Venetian doges on the walls and a Veronese-painted ceiling. The Doge's private rooms, which offer an insight into the everyday routine of Venice's rulers, are also located in the palace. The elegance and sophistication of the Venetian court are reflected in the exquisite furniture, tapestries, and frescoes that adorn these rooms.

The prison, which is connected to the palace by the Bridge of Sighs, is among the most intriguing features of the Doge's Palace. Inmates serving sentences or awaiting trial were housed in the Piombi prison. In sharp contrast to the palace's splendor, the cells are small and dim. The enclosed bridge with tiny windows providing a view of the outside world is called the Bridge of Sighs, and it crosses the Rio di Palazzo canal. The sighs of inmates who crossed the bridge on their way to the jail, enjoying their final view of Venice before being imprisoned, are what gave the bridge its name. It is a moving experience to go across the Bridge of Sighs because it lets you picture the feelings of people who crossed it centuries ago.

Consider taking a guided tour to add even more special memories to your visit to the Doge's Palace and the Bridge of Sighs. Numerous tour operators provide guided tours that cover the history, architecture, and artwork of these sites in great detail. You may better understand the significance of the palace's sculptures, paintings, and other features—as well as Venice's history and culture—by taking a guided tour. Additionally, some excursions provide skip-the-line access, which can help you save time when things become busy. The palace offers audio tours for rent for those who would rather take their time exploring.

It is crucial to remember that there is an admission charge if you intend to enter the Doge's Palace. Tickets are available online or via the Doge's Palace's official website (https://palazzoducale.visitmuve.it). It is advised to purchase tickets in advance in order to avoid long lineups and guarantee your desired time slot, particularly during the busiest travel seasons. To assist you in planning your visit, the website also offers details about special events, opening hours, and other information. You can reach the Doge's Palace at +39 041 2715911 with any questions.

There are a number of other things you may do in the vicinity to improve your experience, aside from touring the Doge's Palace and the Bridge of Sighs. Just outside the palace, Piazza San Marco is a bustling square with many old houses, cafes, and stores. You can enjoy a coffee or a glass of wine at one of the outdoor cafés, such as Caffè Florian or Gran Caffè Quadri, while soaking in the atmosphere and views of the area. Another must-see landmark in Piazza San Marco is the Campanile, also known as the bell tower. It provides sweeping views of Venice and the surrounding lagoon from its approximately 100-meter height. Upon ascending the tower via elevator, visitors can take in breath-taking views over the city's roofs, canals, and islands.

Grand Canal and Rialto Bridge

Two of Venice's most famous and important sights are the Grand Canal and the Rialto Bridge, which are must-sees for anybody traveling through this enchanted city. Together, they provide tourists with an opportunity to experience Venice's distinct charm, beauty, and culture while also serving as a geographical and historical representation of the city's center. The oldest and most well-known bridge over the Grand Canal is the Rialto Bridge, also known as the Ponte di Rialto, which has long served as a representation of Venice. The city's principal waterway, the Grand Canal, often known as Canal Grande, is dotted with magnificent palaces, old structures, and vibrant marketplaces. There are innumerable things to see and do to make your time at these places genuinely unique, and visiting them is an experience that will never be forgotten.

The Rialto Bridge connects the two sides of the Grand Canal and is located in Venice's San Polo and San Marco neighborhoods. It is conveniently accessible from all areas of Venice and is located next to the Rialto Market, one of the oldest and liveliest markets in the city. You may take a vaporetto, or water bus, from the Santa Lucia train station to the Rialto stop, which is only a short stroll from the bridge, if you are traveling to Venice by train. You may take in views of the city's historic structures and the Grand Canal while traveling by vaporetto, which is both convenient and picturesque. If you are coming from Marco Polo Airport, you can book a private water taxi for a quicker and more direct ride, or you can take the Alilaguna water bus to the Rialto stop. Most areas in Venice are accessible by foot from the Rialto Bridge, and the trek itself is delightful as you wind through the city's quaint alleyways and canals.

Renowned for its exquisite design and historical significance, the Rialto Bridge is considered a masterpiece of Renaissance architecture. Earlier wooden bridges that had stood in the same spot were replaced by the present stone bridge, which was finished in 1591. Antonio da Ponte created the bridge, which spans the Grand Canal under a single arch and has two rows of stores lining the central path. These stores, which offer jewelry, trinkets, and other goods, enhance the bridge's vibrant ambiance and draw both tourists and residents. The bridge is a popular location for tourism and photography since it provides breathtaking views of the Grand Canal.

Simply crossing the Rialto Bridge and admiring the Grand Canal is one of the greatest ways to experience it. From the bridge, you may observe the stunning palaces and structures that line the canal's banks, as well as gondolas, vaporettos, and other boats gliding along it. At sunset, when the warm light bounces off the sea and produces a lovely and picturesque landscape, the view is particularly magical. The stores on the bridge are an excellent spot to purchase souvenirs for individuals who enjoy shopping because they provide a wide range of unique things, from Venetian glass to handcrafted jewelry.

The major thoroughfare of Venice, the Grand Canal, is approximately 3.8 kilometers long and is frequently called the "most beautiful street in the world." It forms an S-shape as it flows through the city, connecting the lagoon to the center of Venice. More than 170 ancient structures, many of which are from the 13th and 18th centuries, border the canal, including palaces, churches, and museums. With their elaborate façade and distinctive architectural designs, these structures capture the riches and influence of Venice in its heyday.

Taking a boat ride down the Grand Canal is one of the greatest ways to see it. The vaporetto, which functions similarly to a public bus and makes stops at several locations along the canal, is the most economical and practical choice. Because it runs the whole length of the Grand Canal and provides great views of the city's attractions, Line 1 of the vaporetto is especially well-liked by tourists. You can rent a gondola and take a leisurely trip along the canal for a more private and romantic experience. Gondola rides offer a distinctive viewpoint of the city's beauty and charm and are a classic Venetian experience. For a quicker and more opulent ride, you can also reserve a private water taxi.

There are a number of sites and sights to be aware of while traveling the Grand Canal. Among the most well-known is the Golden House, also known as the Ca' d'Oro, a magnificent house with a recognizable Gothic front. If you have the time, it is worthwhile to visit the palace, which is now a museum with a collection of artwork and relics. The Palazzo Grassi, a magnificent 18th-century mansion that holds exhibitions of modern art, is another noteworthy site. Another must-see destination along the Grand Canal is the Peggy Guggenheim Collection, which is housed at the Palazzo Venier dei Leoni. With pieces by well-known painters like Picasso, Pollock, and Dalí, this museum of modern art provides an intriguing contrast to Venice's old buildings.

Another attraction in the region is the Rialto Market, which is a must-see for foodies and is located next to the Rialto Bridge. Known for its fresh vegetables, seafood, and regional specialties, this lively market has been a hub of trade and commerce for generations. One of the best ways to take in Venice's lively atmosphere and try some of its delectable cuisine is to visit the market. Try some of the regional cuisine, which is served at local eateries and food stands. Examples include risotto al nero di seppia (squid ink risotto) and sarde in saor (sweet and sour sardines).

Consider joining a guided tour to add even more special memories to your trip to the Grand Canal and the Rialto Bridge. Numerous tour organizations provide in-depth information about the history, architecture, and culture of these places through guided walking tours or boat trips. You may better understand the significance of the Grand Canal and the Rialto Bridge, as well as the myths and legends surrounding them, by taking a guided tour. Additionally, some excursions include skip-the-line access to neighboring sites, such St. Mark's Basilica or the Doge's Palace, which can help you save time during peak hours.

It is advised to make reservations in advance for a private boat trip or gondola ride, particularly during the busiest travel seasons. Gondola rides and boat trips can be booked online through a number of tour companies and booking websites, including GetYourGuide and Viator. You can visit their official website (https://www.veneziaunica.it) or call the Venice Tourist Information Office at +39 041 5298711 with any questions or concerns.

Hidden Gems and Off-the-Beaten-Path Spots

Acqua Alta Library

Known as "The Floating Bookstore," Libreria Acqua Alta is one of Venice's most distinctive and alluring hidden treasures. This eccentric bookshop, which is hidden away in a peaceful area of the city, is a must-see for bookworms, photographers, and anybody else looking for a unique Venice experience. In contrast to conventional bookshops, Libreria Acqua Alta imaginatively keeps its books in bathtubs, waterproof bins, and even gondolas to meet the challenges of Venice's periodic flooding, or "acqua alta." This imaginative method has made the bookstore famous all over the world by creating a magical and unforgettable atmosphere in addition to protecting the books from water damage. Discovering a world of originality, charm, and Venetian inventiveness is what visiting Libreria Acqua Alta is all about.

The Castello neighborhood of Venice is home to Libreria Acqua Alta, which is close to Campo Santa Maria Formosa and only a short stroll from St. Mark's Square. Calle Longa Santa Maria Formosa, 5176/B, 30122 Venice, Italy is the precise address. Because it is nestled away in a small alley that is easy to overlook, the bookstore maintains its intimate and secret vibe despite its increasing popularity. You may walk to the bookstore from either the Rialto stop or the San Zaccaria stop, where you can get a vaporetto (water bus). It takes roughly ten minutes to walk through the picturesque streets of Venice from the Rialto stop, and fifteen minutes from the San Zaccaria stop. The bookstore is conveniently located on foot if you are staying in the Castello or San Marco neighborhoods, and the trip itself is delightful as you wind your way through Venice's charming streets and canals.

The imaginative and unusual interior design of Libreria Acqua Alta is among its most striking attributes. In an arrangement that is both disorganized and captivating, the bookstore is brimming with a diverse array of new and secondhand books, periodicals, maps, and prints. The books are kept in gondolas, bathtubs, barrels, and other waterproof containers rather than conventional shelves, which not only keeps them safe from floods but also contributes to the store's distinct appeal. The bookstore's focal point is a large, book-filled gondola that occupies the center of the main area. Together with the other unique storage options, this gondola makes Libreria Acqua Alta a genuinely unique place to visit.

You will find a number of tiny chambers and corners around the bookstore, many of which are brimming with hidden gems just waiting to be found. Books spanning a variety of subjects, including literature, history, art, and travel, are included in the collection in several languages. Along with odd and quirky treasures that make excellent keepsakes, there are also rare and ancient books. Every area of the store offers a different and picturesque scene, making Libreria Acqua Alta a photographer's paradise. It feels as though you've entered a storybook thanks to the books, gondolas, and the warm, little chaotic ambiance.

The outdoor space at the rear of Libreria Acqua Alta, which has a stairway composed completely of used books, is one of the highlights of the visit. Visitors can take in a glimpse of the canal behind the bookstore from the little platform that is reached by this "book staircase." Climbing the stairway is a necessity for anyone visiting Libreria Acqua Alta, as it has become one of the store's most recognizable and photographed features. The store's appeal is enhanced by a gondola moored in the canal and a little dining area outside where you can unwind and take in the ambience.

Libreria Acqua Alta's proximity to Venice's canals is another distinctive aspect of the establishment. The bookstore's back entrance opens right into a canal, and occasionally, at high tide, water runs inside the store, producing a wonderful and strange scene. The store's authenticity and character are enhanced by its close proximity to the canals, which serves as a reminder of both the difficulties and the beauties of living in Venice. The tranquil atmosphere of this undiscovered area of the city is widely enjoyed by visitors who sit along the canal and watch the gondolas go by.

Spend some time perusing the selection and selecting a few books to bring home as mementos to enhance your trip to Libreria Acqua Alta. You will undoubtedly find something remarkable, whether you are searching for a classic novel, a Venice guidebook, or a one-of-a-kind work of art. Additionally, postcards, prints, and other little items that make excellent presents or mementos are available for purchase at the bookstore. If you're lucky, you might even get to meet the store's amiable resident cats, who contribute to the warm and inviting ambiance.

There is no admission charge to Libreria Acqua Alta, and reservations are not required. The store might grow crowded later in the day, especially during the busiest travel seasons, so it's best to visit in the morning or early afternoon. The bookstore's regular hours are 9:00 AM to 8:00 PM, however it's a good idea to check ahead of time because they might change. For questions or more details, call +39 041 2960841 to reach Libreria Acqua Alta. Although there isn't an official website for the bookstore, you can discover reviews and information on travel websites like Google Maps and TripAdvisor.

To improve your experience, you can engage in a number of additional local activities in addition to touring Libreria Acqua Alta. One of the most genuine and less visited areas of Venice is the Castello district, where the bookstore is located. It provides an insight into the everyday lives of Venetians. Campo Santa Maria Formosa, a quaint area with a lovely church and a number of cafés where you can unwind and have a snack or coffee, is one of the nearby attractions. Another must-see location is the Rialto Market, which is only a short stroll from the bookstore and serves local specialties, fish, and fresh produce.

Calm Squares and Neighborhood Churches

Beyond the well-traveled routes, Venice has a more serene, private side that is just as captivating. The city is known for its imposing landmarks, busy canals, and famous attractions. Quiet squares called "campi" and neighborhood churches may be found all across Venice, providing a tranquil haven from the bustle and an opportunity to take in the genuine charm of Venetian life. Tourists frequently ignore these hidden gems, but those who wish to discover the city's lesser-known treasures should not miss them because of their rich history, culture, and beauty. You can travel back in time, take in the breathtaking architecture, and establish a profound and intimate connection with Venice's soul by visiting these peaceful squares and neighborhood churches.

Venice's system of campi, or little squares where residents congregate, is one of its most endearing features. These squares have a calm, relaxed vibe and are frequently hidden away in residential areas, in contrast to the magnificent Piazza San Marco. The Dorsoduro district's Campo Santa Margherita is one such square. Lined with cafés, restaurants, and small stores, this busy yet laid-back area is a popular with locals, particularly students from the nearby university. It is the perfect place to sit and observe everyday life while sipping coffee or a spritz. You can take a vaporetto to the Ca' Rezzonico stop and walk for roughly five minutes to reach Campo Santa Margherita. Additionally, it's easy to walk from other portions of San Polo and Dorsoduro to the square.

The Santa Croce district's Campo San Giacomo dell'Orio is another undiscovered treasure. With kids playing, senior citizens conversing on benches, and a few tiny eateries offering authentic Venetian fare, this area has a decidedly local vibe. One of Venice's oldest churches, the Church of San Giacomo dell'Orio, was built in the ninth century and is located on the plaza. The church's elaborate interior, which includes stunning paintings, a wooden roof that resembles a ship's hull, and an amazing altarpiece by Lorenzo Lotto, stands in stark contrast to its plain façade. You can take a vaporetto to the Riva de Biasio stop and walk for roughly ten minutes to get to Campo San Giacomo dell'Orio. You get a peek of daily life in Venice as you travel through serene streets and canals.

Another serene square that is worth seeing is Campo San Barnaba, which is located in the Dorsoduro area. The Church of San Barnaba, with its neoclassical façade and intriguing history, dominates this little square. Although religious services are no longer held in the church, it frequently hosts cultural events and art exhibits. The church was included in a notable sequence in the film Indiana Jones and the Last Crusade, so fans may know it. With a tiny canal flowing alongside it and a few outdoor cafés, the square itself is a great spot to unwind. Take a vaporetto to the Ca' Rezzonico stop and walk for around five minutes to reach Campo San Barnaba.

Venice is home to numerous local churches that are architectural and artistic marvels in addition to these squares. Santa Maria dei Miracoli, which is located in the Cannaregio neighborhood, is one such church. With a façade composed completely of polychrome marble, this modest but elegant church is a marvel of Renaissance architecture. The church's interior is as magnificent, including elaborate carvings, a vaulted ceiling, and a serene atmosphere that makes it the ideal spot for introspection. Known as the "marble church," Santa Maria dei Miracoli is a popular venue for weddings and other special events in Venice. Walk for roughly ten minutes through the picturesque streets of Cannaregio after taking a vaporetto to the Fondamente Nove stop to get to the church.

Located in the Castello neighborhood on the island of San Pietro, San Pietro di Castello is another outstanding church. With an interesting history that stretches back to the 7th century, this building was the cathedral of Venice until St. Mark's Basilica replaced it. The church offers a tranquil escape from the bustling areas of the city because it is encircled by a serene, green square. Beautiful artwork may be found within, such as a Veronese painting and a marble throne that is claimed to have been used by St. Peter. Take a vaporetto to the

San Pietro stop and walk for around five minutes to reach San Pietro di Castello.

The Church of San Sebastiano in the Dorsoduro area is a hidden treasure that history and art buffs should not pass over. The interior of this cathedral is adorned with beautiful murals, paintings, and altarpieces created by the Venetian painter Paolo Veronese, whose creations are a veritable gold mine. Visitors are able to completely enjoy the magnificence of Veronese's work without being distracted by big crowds because the church is very modest and frequently quiet. Take a vaporetto to the San Basilio stop and then walk for roughly ten minutes to get to San Sebastiano.

In addition to taking in their beauty, visiting these peaceful squares and neighborhood churches offers a chance to learn more about Venice's past and culture. As hubs of daily life, places of worship, and gathering places, many of these locations have been an integral part of their communities for generations. You may learn more about what makes Venice so exceptional and one-of-a-kind by spending time in these obscure areas of the city.

Consider going on a guided walking tour that highlights Venice's lesser-known sights and hidden treasures if you want to get the most out of your trip. Numerous tour companies provide private or small-group tours that stop at local churches and peaceful squares and offer detailed information about their architecture, history, and significance. These tours frequently incorporate anecdotes and stories that make the locations come to life and enhance your experience. It might be difficult to traverse Venice's winding streets if you like to explore alone, so pack a good map or use a navigation app.

While some churches may request a nominal payment to aid in upkeep and repair, the majority of the squares and churches listed do not charge admission. Tickets are typically available on-site or via the official websites of churches that hold special events or art exhibitions. For instance, you can find details about events, tickets, and opening hours on the Church of San Sebastiano's website (https://www.chorusvenezia.org). The Venice Tourist Information Office can be reached at +39 041 5298711 or on their official website (https://www.veneziaunica.it) if you need help or have any inquiries.

Courtyards and Hidden Gardens

Venice is renowned for its historic buildings, canals, and bridges, but beneath its imposing exterior and winding alleys is a world of secret courtyards and gardens that provide a peaceful respite from the busy streets. Tourists frequently ignore these undiscovered green areas, despite the fact that they are among the city's most charming and serene locations. These courtyards and gardens, many of which are hidden away in old structures, monasteries, or private mansions, offer a window into a more sedate and private side of Venice. A unique approach to take in the beauty and history of the city is to visit these hidden courtyards and gardens, which also provide you a peaceful, intimate connection with Venice.

The garden of Palazzo Querini Stampalia, which is located in the Castello neighborhood close to St. Mark's Square, is one of Venice's most well-known hidden gardens. The modern garden created by famed architect Carlo Scarpa is the hidden treasure of this old palace, which also houses a museum, library, and cultural foundation. The garden, which has stone walkways, water channels, and an abundance of flora, is a tasteful fusion of modern and traditional Venetian design. It is a tranquil haven where guests may unwind and take in the beauty of the thoughtfully chosen plants as well as the sound of trickling water. You can take a vaporetto to the San Zaccaria stop and walk for roughly five minutes to get to Palazzo Querini Stampalia. The public is welcome to visit the museum and garden, and tickets are available online or in person at https://www.querinistampalia.org. You can reach the foundation at +39 041 2711411 with any questions.

The Peggy Guggenheim Collection's garden, which is located along the Grand Canal in the Dorsoduro neighborhood, is another undiscovered gem. The garden of this modern art museum, which is located in the Palazzo Venier dei Leoni, is a calm and lovely area with trees, flowers, and sculptures. The garden serves as a peaceful haven where guests can rest and think in addition to being a place to view artwork. It is especially noteworthy since Peggy Guggenheim's ashes are interred there with her cherished dogs, in what was formerly her private garden. Take a vaporetto to the Accademia stop and walk for around five minutes to arrive at the Peggy Guggenheim Collection. Access to the garden is included in museum admission tickets, which may be purchased online at the official website (https://www.guggenheim-venice.it). You can reach the museum at +39 041 2405411 for additional details.

The garden of the Jewish Museum of Venice is located in the old Jewish Ghetto in the Cannaregio neighborhood. This little but significant garden honors the Holocaust victims and serves as a space for introspection and memory. It has a serene green area with benches and trees, as well as a memorial wall bearing the names of Venetian Jews who were deported during World War II. The garden is a peaceful, reflective area that provides a greater comprehension of Venice's past and the tenacity of its Jewish population. Take a vaporetto to the Guglie stop and walk for around five minutes to get to the Jewish Museum. Access to the garden is included with museum admission tickets, which are available on-site or online at https://www.museoebraico.it. You can reach the museum at +39 041 715359 with any questions.

The garden of the Monastery of San Francesco della Vigna, which is located in the Castello neighborhood of Venice, is one of the city's most charming hidden gardens. There is a lovely, peaceful garden with citrus trees, flowers, and herbs at this old monastery. The Franciscan monks who reside in the monastery look after the garden, which is a haven of spirituality and tranquility. The park and the nearby church, which has beautiful architecture and artwork, are open to visitors. Take a vaporetto to the Celestia stop and walk for approximately five minutes to get to San Francesco della Vigna. It is essential to inquire with the monastery about the exact hours when the garden is open to tourists. You can reach the monastery at +39 041 5280415, for additional information.

Venice is home to other secret courtyards that are just as fascinating as these well-known gardens. These courtyards, which frequently include lovely architecture, fountains, and flora, are found inside ancient buildings or private mansions. The Corte del Milion, which is close to the Rialto Bridge, is one such courtyard. Marco Polo is rumored to have lived in this serene and charming courtyard, which is a great place to stop and enjoy the ambience of historic Venice. Take a vaporetto to the Rialto stop and walk for around five minutes to arrive at the Corte del Milion.

The Corte Botera, in the San Polo neighborhood, is another lovely courtyard. This hidden gem has a little well in the middle that was originally utilized by locals to gather water, and it is flanked by old houses. The courtyard is a serene, picturesque area that transports one to a bygone era. Take a vaporetto to the San Silvestro stop and walk for around five minutes to get to the Corte Botera.

Discovering Venice's hidden courtyards and gardens offers more than just the chance to take in the beauty of the city; it also provides an opportunity to gain knowledge of its culture and history. Many of these areas provide a window into the past and current lives of Venetians and have been meticulously conserved and maintained for centuries. You may uncover a side of Venice that is frequently missed but no less captivating by taking the time to explore these little-known areas of the city.

Consider going on a guided walking tour that highlights Venice's secret courtyards and gardens to get the most out of your trip. Numerous tour operators provide private or small-group trips that visit these hidden locations and offer comprehensive details on its significance, history, and design. These tours are a special and intimate experience because they frequently grant entry to private gardens that are closed to the public. It might be difficult to traverse Venice's winding streets if you like to explore alone, so pack a good map or use a navigation app.

Although some may request a nominal gift to aid in upkeep and restoration, the majority of the gardens and courtyards featured do not charge admission. Tickets for gardens owned by museums or other cultural organizations are typically available on-site or via their official websites. The Venice Tourist Information Office can be reached at +39 041 5298711 or on their official website (https://www.veneziaunica.it) if you need help or have any inquiries.

Galleries and Museums of Art

Guggenheim Collection by Peggy

One of the most well-known museums in Venice is the Peggy Guggenheim Collection, which is a must-see for anybody interested in modern art. This museum is housed in the Palazzo

Venier dei Leoni, a famous 18th-century structure that was formerly the residence of Peggy Guggenheim, a prominent art patron and collector, and is located along the Grand Canal in the Dorsoduro area. With pieces by some of the finest modern artists, the collection is among the most significant in Italy for European and American contemporary art from the first half of the 20th century. Discovering more about the life and legacy of Peggy Guggenheim, who was instrumental in forming the contemporary art world, is another benefit of visiting the Peggy Guggenheim Collection in addition to taking in the amazing artwork.

Palazzo Venier dei Leoni, 701 Dorsoduro, 30123 Venice, Italy is the address of the museum. It is conveniently accessible from many locations throughout the city due to its location along the Grand Canal. The nearest stop for those arriving by vaporetto (water bus) is Accademia, which is serviced by Line 1. The museum is within a five-minute walk from the Accademia stop. The Salute stop is also close by, and you can take a vaporetto there instead. The museum is roughly a fifteen-minute walk from St. Mark's Square, via the Accademia Bridge and the quaint alleyways of Dorsoduro. The museum is easily accessible by foot if you are lodging in the Dorsoduro neighborhood, and the trip itself is enjoyable as you wind through Venice's charming lanes and canals.

Paintings, sculptures, and other pieces by some of the most significant artists of the 20th century are among the outstanding collection of contemporary art that is the Peggy Guggenheim Collection. Masterworks by artists such Pablo

Picasso, Jackson Pollock, Salvador Dalí, Joan Miró, Wassily Kandinsky, and Max Ernst—who was also Peggy Guggenheim's second husband—are included in the collection. The palazzo's rooms, which still have the cozy atmosphere of a private residence, are used to display the museum's permanent collection. Visitors can interact with the art in a more intimate and captivating way in this special location, almost like if they were staying at Peggy Guggenheim's home.

Jackson Pollock's Alchemy, a seminal piece that perfectly captures the artist's inventive drip painting style, is one of the collection's highlights. One of the numerous artists that Peggy Guggenheim encouraged was Pollock, whose artwork is prominently shown in the museum. The Empire of Light, a bizarre and provocative painting by René Magritte that captivates the mind, is another noteworthy work. In addition, visitors can view sculptures by artists like Alberto Giacometti and Constantin Brâncuși, as well as pieces by Piet Mondrian, including his well-known geometric compositions.

The museum has temporary exhibitions that feature pieces by various modern and contemporary artists in addition to its permanent collection. These shows, which frequently feature works on loan from other esteemed institutions, offer a chance to investigate various facets of modern art. Even for returning visitors, the museum's schedule of temporary exhibitions guarantees that there is always something fresh and fascinating to see.

The Peggy Guggenheim Collection's outdoor areas are yet another feature. With pieces by artists like Henry Moore, Alexander Calder, and Jean Arp, the sculpture garden—also called the Nasher Sculpture Garden—is a serene and lovely setting. Surrounded by nature and art, the garden is the ideal spot to unwind and think. Additionally, it is particularly significant since Peggy Guggenheim's ashes are interred there with those of her cherished dogs, marking their final resting place. The garden is a noteworthy aspect of the museum experience because of its serene ambiance and magnificent sculptures.

The Peggy Guggenheim Collection's setting along the Grand Canal is among its most distinctive features. Beautiful views of the canal and the other palaces can be seen from the museum's terrace, which makes it the ideal location for photos. In addition to the famous dome of the Basilica di Santa Maria della Salute in the distance, visitors may take in the sight of gondolas and vaporettos floating down the lake. The terrace is a great place to stop and enjoy Venice's splendor while thinking about the museum's artwork and history.

Think about going on a guided trip to the Peggy Guggenheim Collection to enhance your experience. The museum provides in-depth information about the artworks, the artists, and the life and legacy of Peggy Guggenheim through guided tours given by knowledgeable staff. You can learn more about the collection and the setting in which it was made by taking one of these tours. For individuals who would rather take their time exploring the museum, audio guides are also offered. The museum provides unique courses and activities for families with kids that are intended to keep them interested and expose them to the world of modern art.

With the exception of Tuesdays and some holidays, the Peggy Guggenheim Collection is accessible to the public every day. Tickets can be bought online at https://www.guggenheim-venice.it, the museum's official website, or in person. It is advised to purchase tickets in advance in order to avoid the line and guarantee your desired time slot, particularly during the busiest travel seasons. Additionally, the website offers details on special events, temporary exhibitions, and opening hours. The museum's phone number is +39 041 2405411, and its email address is info@guggenheim-venice.it.

To improve your experience, you can do a number of additional things nearby in addition to touring the museum. The Dorsoduro neighborhood is well-known for its thriving art scene, quaint lanes, and top-notch dining options. The Basilica di Santa Maria della Salute, a magnificent Baroque church and one of Venice's most recognizable structures, is a nearby attraction, as is the Gallerie dell'Accademia, which has an impressive collection of Venetian Renaissance artwork. Numerous tiny galleries, artisan stores, and cafés where you may unwind and take in the local ambience can also be found in the region.

Gallery of the Academy

Anyone interested in Venice's rich artistic legacy should make time to visit the Gallerie dell'Accademia, one of the city's most renowned art museums. This museum, which is close to the southern end of the Accademia Bridge in the Dorsoduro area, has an impressive collection of Venetian art that spans several centuries. It gives guests the opportunity to view works from earlier and later eras as well as masterpieces by some of the best artists of the Venetian Renaissance and Baroque periods. The Gallerie dell'Accademia is more than just a museum; it's a voyage through Venice's history as seen by its most gifted sculptors and painters. A deeper understanding of Venice's artistic and cultural heritage can be gained by visiting this museum, which is an experience that will never be forgotten.

Campo della Carità, Dorsoduro 1050, 30123 Venice, Italy is the address of the museum. It is conveniently accessible from many locations throughout the city due to its proximity to the Grand Canal and the Accademia Bridge. The nearest stop for those arriving by vaporetto (water bus) is Accademia, which is serviced by Lines 1 and 2. The museum is only a short stroll from the Accademia stop. The museum is accessible from St. Mark's Square via the Accademia Bridge, which provides breathtaking views of the Grand Canal. It takes roughly ten to fifteen minutes to walk from St. Mark's Square. The museum is easily accessible by foot for visitors staying in the Dorsoduro district, and the trip itself is enjoyable as you pass through the quaint squares and lanes of this creative district.

The Gallerie dell'Accademia is well known for its vast collection of Venetian artwork, which spans the 14th through the 18th century and includes paintings, sculptures, and drawings. The Accademia di Belle Arti, Venice's Academy of Fine Arts, had its headquarters in a historic complex that was once a monastery and now houses the museum's collection. The structure itself is a masterwork of Venetian design, including roomy galleries and exquisite embellishments that give the artworks on exhibit a sophisticated backdrop.

The museum's collection of paintings by Giovanni Bellini, one of the most significant Venetian Renaissance painters, is one of its attractions. Bellini's paintings offer an intriguing window into the creative advancements of his day and are praised for their brilliant hues, fine details, and emotional depth. Masterworks like The Madonna and Child and The Feast of the Gods, which display Bellini's talent for portraying the beauty of the natural world and the human soul, are on display for visitors to appreciate.

The museum's collection of paintings by Titian, one of the greatest High Renaissance painters, is another popular draw. Titian's paintings have had a significant impact on art history and are renowned for their dramatic compositions, vibrant colors, and strong emotions. The Presentation of the Virgin in the Temple, a colossal painting that showcases Titian's command of perspective and narrative, is one of the collection's masterpieces.

Tintoretto, another imposing figure in Venetian painting, has a number of famous pieces at the Gallerie dell'Accademia. Intense energy, daring use of light and shadow, and dramatic compositions are characteristics of Tintoretto's works. Works like The Miracle of the Slave, which depicts a dramatic moment with amazing emotion and detail, are on display for visitors to appreciate. The inventiveness and inventiveness of Venetian artists throughout the Renaissance are demonstrated by Tintoretto's paintings.

The museum's collection also features pieces by other well-known artists like Veronese, Giorgione, Carpaccio, and Canaletto. While Giorgione's paintings are renowned for their poetic and enigmatic elements, Veronese's paintings are praised for their grandeur and opulence. Renaissance Venice's life and culture are vividly shown in Carpaccio's narrative paintings, while Canaletto's meticulous observations of the city flawlessly convey its beauty and allure.

Leonardo da Vinci's Vitruvian Man, a drawing that has come to represent the Renaissance, is among the most well-known pieces in the museum. Due to its fragility, this masterpiece—which captures the ideal proportions of the human body—is rarely shown, but it is a member of the museum's collection and is occasionally on display at special occasions. Those who are fortunate enough to view this drawing in person are in for a unique and memorable experience.

The layout of the museum's galleries enables visitors to see how Venetian art evolved throughout time, from its Gothic origins to its Renaissance and Baroque peaks. Every area has been thoughtfully chosen to emphasize the distinctive qualities of the artworks as well as the historical setting in which they were produced. Additionally, the museum hosts temporary exhibitions that highlight pieces from other collections or delve deeper into particular subjects. The chance to view significant and uncommon pieces of art that are not in the permanent collection is offered by these exhibitions.

A guided tour is a great way to enhance your experience at the Gallerie dell'Accademia. The museum provides in-depth information on the artworks, the creators, and the history of Venetian art through guided tours conducted by knowledgeable art historians. The collection and the cultural setting in which it was produced can be better understood with the help of these excursions. For individuals who would rather take their time exploring the museum, audio guides are also offered. In order to engage young visitors and introduce them to the world of art, the museum provides special programs and events for families with children.

With the exception of several holidays, the Gallerie dell'Accademia is available to the public every day. Tickets are available online at https://www.gallerieaccademia.it, the museum's official website, or in person. It is advised to purchase tickets in advance in order to avoid the line and guarantee your desired time slot, particularly during the busiest travel seasons. Additionally, the website offers details on special events, temporary exhibitions, and opening hours.

You can email the museum at info@gallerieaccademia.it or call +39 041 5222247 with any questions.

To improve your experience, you can do a number of additional things nearby in addition to touring the museum. The Dorsoduro neighborhood is well-known for its thriving art scene, quaint lanes, and top-notch dining options. The Basilica di Santa Maria della Salute, a magnificent Baroque church and one of Venice's most recognizable monuments, and the Peggy Guggenheim Collection, which houses an exceptional collection of modern art, are nearby attractions. Numerous tiny galleries, artisan stores, and cafés where you may unwind and take in the local ambience can also be found in the region.

Museo Correr

One of Venice's most comprehensive and fascinating museums, the Museo Correr gives visitors a close-up look at the city's rich art, history, and culture. The museum is housed in the Napoleonic Wing and a portion of the Procuratie Nuove, two imposing structures that constitute the square's western and southern borders. It is located in St. Mark's Square, in the center of Venice. Anyone interested in learning about Venice's history, from its beginnings as a strong maritime republic to its artistic and cultural accomplishments, must visit the Museo Correr, which is a component of the Venice Civic Museums network. The museum tells the narrative of Venice and its people through a journey through time, not merely a collection of relics and artwork.

One of the easiest places to see in Venice is the museum, which is located at 52 Piazza San Marco, 30124, Italy. The nearest stops for those arriving by vaporetto (water bus) are San Marco Vallaresso and San Zaccaria, which are both serviced by Lines 1 and 2. The museum is located in St. Mark's Square, which is only a short stroll from either stop. The museum is easily accessible if you are already in the vicinity because it is next to the Campanile (bell tower) and just across from St. Mark's Basilica. Whether you are touring the area or going to neighboring attractions like the Doge's Palace or the Bridge of Sighs, its central location makes it a convenient complement to any itinerary.

Teodoro Correr, a wealthy Venetian nobleman and art collector who left his vast collection to the city in the early 1800s, is honored by the name of the Museo Correr. His collection served as the museum's starting point, and it has subsequently expanded to house a variety of exhibits addressing many facets of Venetian art, history, and culture. The museum's galleries, which are arranged thematically and span multiple floors, let visitors examine various eras and aspects of Venice's history.

The collection of Venetian art in the Museo Correr, which spans the Middle Ages to the 19th century and includes paintings, sculptures, and decorative arts, is one of its attractions. Some of the most significant Venetian artists, such as Vittore Carpaccio, Giovanni Bellini, and Canova, are represented in the museum's art collection. Bellini's religious paintings demonstrate his command of color and arrangement, while Carpaccio's narrative paintings, such The Two Venetian

Ladies, offer a striking window into the daily life and culture of Renaissance Venice. Antonio Canova, one of the best neoclassical sculptors, has a number of sculptures at the museum that are praised for their beauty and emotional depth. The Museo Correr is home to a vast collection of historical objects that provide insight into Venice's political, social, and cultural past in addition to its art collection. Maps, records, coins, and other artifacts that depict the emergence and collapse of the Venetian Republic can be found in the museum's historical department. Visitors can discover more about the city's trading networks, maritime might, and distinctive political structure, which was headed by the Great Council and the Doge. With displays on furniture, clothes, and other facets of material culture, the museum also delves into Venetian daily life.

Empress Elisabeth of Austria, also known as Sisi, used the Imperial Rooms, one of the most striking features of the Museo Correr, when she visited Venice in the 1800s. These exquisitely furnished neoclassical chambers offer a window into the lavish way of life enjoyed by European aristocrats. Because they blend historical value with architectural and artistic splendor, the Imperial Rooms are a popular destination for tourists.

The history of St. Mark's Square, one of Venice's most recognizable and important historical sites, is also covered in the museum. This section examines the square's architectural development, its function as a hub of social and political activity, and its metamorphosis into a representation of

Venice's identity. Models, sketches, and images that chronicle the square's history and significance to the city are on display for visitors.

Consider going on a guided tour to enhance the experience of your visit to the Museo Correr. Guided tours are available at the museum, with experienced staff members offering in-depth explanations of the exhibitions, Venice's history, and the backstories of the artwork and objects. These tours are a great opportunity to learn more about the museum's holdings and the cultural setting in which they were produced. For individuals who would rather take their time exploring the museum, audio guides are also offered. The museum provides unique programs and activities for families with kids that are intended to keep them interested and introduce them to Venice's history and culture.

With the exception of several holidays, the Museo Correr is available to the public every day. Tickets are available online at https://www.visitmuve.it, the museum's official website, or in person. It is advised to purchase tickets in advance in order to avoid the line and guarantee your desired time slot, particularly during the busiest travel seasons. Additionally, the website offers details on special events, temporary exhibitions, and opening hours. The museum can be reached by phone at +39 041 2405211 or via email at info@fmcvenezia.it.

Visitors can enrich their experience by touring other neighboring sites that are a member of the Venice Civic Museums network in addition to touring the Museo Correr.

These include the National Archaeological Museum, which has an amazing collection of ancient relics, and the Doge's Palace, which provides an intriguing glimpse at Venice's political and judicial past. These museums offer bundled tickets that let guests experience several attractions at a reduced cost. For individuals who wish to maximize their time in St. Mark's Square and gain a deeper understanding of Venice's history and culture, this ticket is an excellent choice. Spend some time exploring St. Mark's Square and the surrounding area once you've finished your visit to the Museo Correr. With its magnificent architecture, vibrant atmosphere, and breathtaking views of the Basilica and the Campanile, the square is among Venice's most exquisite and recognizable locations. You may also take a gondola ride along the canals for a distinctive view of the city, or you can visit the Bridge of Sighs, which links the old jail with the Doge's Palace.

Venetian Islands

Murano

Known as the "Glassmaking Island," Murano is one of the most well-known and intriguing islands in the Venetian Lagoon. A must-see location for any visitor to Venice is Murano, which is well-known throughout the world for its centuries-old glassmaking heritage. About 1.5 kilometers north of Venice, this little island—or rather, a group of islands joined by bridges—offers a distinctive fusion of craftsmanship, art, and history. In addition to taking in the stunning glass sculptures, a trip to Murano offers the opportunity to discover the allure of a more sedate and genuine side of Venice, away from the bustle of the main city. The island has a rich history and is a delightful site to explore because of its colorful buildings, ancient landmarks, and small canals.

It is not too difficult to get to Murano, which is located in the northern section of the Venetian Lagoon. The vaporetto, Venice's public water bus, is the most popular means of transportation to Murano. Venice and Murano are connected by a number of vaporetto lines, the most direct of which are Lines 4.1 and 4.2. These lines take roughly ten to fifteen minutes to go to Murano from Fondamente Nove, a vaporetto stop on Venice's northern coast. Line 3, which provides a direct connection to Murano and takes about 25 minutes, is an option if you are close to St. Mark's Square. Line 4.2 is a handy choice for people coming from Piazzale Roma or the train station. As you glide across the lagoon and enjoy views of Venice and the neighboring islands, the trip to Murano is picturesque and delightful. Although they are much more costly than the vaporetto, private water taxis are also an option for individuals who want a quicker and more individualized form of transportation.

The most well-known aspect of Murano is its late 13th-century glassmaking heritage. To lower the danger of fires in the main city and to safeguard the trade secrets of glassmakers, the Venetian Republic ordered all of them to relocate their furnaces to Murano in 1291. Murano developed into a glassmaking hub over the ages, creating beautiful glassware that was in great demand throughout Europe. The island is still a major producer of glass today, and tourists can see this age-old art form up close by seeing the numerous glass factories and workshops dotting Murano.

Seeing glassblowers in action is one of the joys of a trip to Murano. Numerous glass manufacturers provide live demonstrations in which talented craftspeople use age-old methods to form molten glass into elaborate items. Observing these demonstrations is intriguing and deepens one's understanding of the creativity and expertise required in glassmaking. The history of Murano glass and the numerous methods used to make different kinds of glassware are also covered in guided tours that are offered by some manufacturers. Even though a lot of these shows are free, it's common to peruse the factory's shop afterwards, where you may buy genuine Murano glass souvenirs. To ensure the product's legitimacy, make sure to search for the genuine Murano Glass trademark.

Another must-see destination in Murano is the Glass Museum, often known as the Museo del Vetro. The museum offers a thorough account of the history of glassmaking on the island and is housed in the Palazzo Giustinian, a historic structure that served as the residence of the Torcello bishops. Its collection demonstrates the development of glassmaking methods and styles over the ages, encompassing ancient Roman glass, medieval and Renaissance pieces, and modern pieces. Visitors of all ages can enjoy an instructive and enriching experience at the museum, which also has exhibits on the science and technology of glass manufacture. The Glass Museum is only a short stroll from the Murano Museo stop, where you can ride the vaporetto to get there. On-site or online ticket sales are available via the official website (https://www.visitmuve.it). You can reach the museum at +39 041 739586 with any questions.

Murano has a rich history of glassmaking and is home to a number of interesting historical sites. One of the most significant churches on the island is the Basilica dei Santi Maria e Donato, a masterwork of Venetian-Byzantine architecture. The magnificent mosaic floor of the basilica, which dates to the 7th century, is renowned for its elaborate geometric designs and animal themes. The church is a center of immense spiritual and historical value, and it also contains relics of Saint Donatus. San Pietro Martire is another well-known church on the island, and it has exquisite paintings by Venetian artists Paolo Veronese and Giovanni Bellini.

Exploring Murano's alleyways and canals is a delight, and the laid-back vibe of the island makes it the ideal spot for a leisurely walk. Charming squares like Campo Santo Stefano, which is home to a remarkable glass sculpture by artist Simone Cenedese, can be found throughout Murano. From intricate chandeliers and sculptures to delicate jewelry and ornaments, the island is home to a wide range of stores and galleries where you can view and buy Murano glass goods. Make sure to stop by a few of the smaller, family-run workshops, where you can discover one-of-a-kind, handcrafted items that showcase the individual style of the craftsman.

Some seminars on Murano include hands-on experiences where guests can try their hand at crafting their own glass pieces for those who wish to learn more about the craft. In addition to creating a unique memento to bring home, these courses offer an enjoyable and engaging opportunity to engage with the island's history. These experiences typically require reservations in advance, and details are frequently available on the websites of specific workshops or through regional tour companies.

Additionally, Murano offers a variety of eateries and cafés where you may savor a meal or a beverage while admiring the island's stunning surroundings. Many of these restaurants offer a flavor of the local cuisine by serving classic Venetian meals and fresh fish. A unique experience that to the allure of your trip to Murano is dining by the water while taking in views of the canals and passing boats.

Think about combining your visit to Murano with stops at other neighboring islands in the Venetian Lagoon, such Burano and Torcello, to get the most out of your trip. Torcello is renowned for its historic churches and serene ambiance, while Burano is famed for its vibrant homes and lace-making customs. These islands are connected by vaporetto lines, which make it simple to visit several locations in a same day.

Torcello: A Calm Retreat

Known as a "Peaceful Escape," Torcello is one of the Venetian Lagoon's most tranquil and historically significant islands. The peaceful town of Torcello, which is roughly 10 kilometers northeast of Venice, gives tourists the opportunity to travel back in time and discover the beginnings of Venetian civilization. Torcello has enormous historical and cultural significance, while being far less populous and developed than other islands like Murano and Burano. Its history began in the 5th century when refugees seeking protection from mainland barbarian invasions sought sanctuary in the lagoon, making it one of the first islands in the lagoon to be inhabited. Before Venice itself rose to prominence, Torcello developed into a flourishing hub of trade and culture. Today, it is a tranquil haven where tourists may explore historic sites, take in the lagoon's natural beauty, and get away from the bustle of the major metropolis.

Torcello is located close to the islands of Burano and Mazzorbo in the northern section of the Venetian Lagoon. It's not too difficult to get to Torcello, and the trip is part of the experience because you can take in the lagoon's natural splendor. The vaporetto, Venice's public water bus, is the most popular means of transportation to Torcello. Starting in Fondamente Nove, a stop on Venice's northern outskirts, Vaporetto Line 12 travels to Torcello with stops at Murano and Burano. A transfer to a smaller vaporetto at Burano completes the quick trip to Torcello, which takes around fifty minutes from Venice. The trip to Torcello just takes five minutes if you are already on Burano. Although they are much more costly than the vaporetto, water taxis offer a choice for individuals who want a quicker and more private ride. Because it provides breathtaking views of the lagoon, its islands, and the surrounding natural landscape, the drive to Torcello is a highlight in and of itself.

The Basilica di Santa Maria Assunta is a magnificent church that was built in 639 AD and is one of the primary attractions in Torcello. This basilica is a masterpiece of Byzantine architecture and one of the oldest buildings in the Venetian Lagoon. Beautiful mosaics, some of the best in Italy, adorn its interior. The Last Judgment mosaic, which fills an entire wall and portrays a striking and dramatic scene of heaven and hell, is the most well-known of them. The mosaics offer an insight into the artistic and theological traditions of the early Venetian settlers and are notable for their fine craftsmanship, vivid colors, and spiritual importance. Additionally, visitors can ascend the basilica's bell tower, which provides stunning sweeping views of Torcello, the lagoon, and the far-off skyline of Venice. The vista from the summit is among the most unforgettable sights on the island, making the trek well worth the effort.

The Church of Santa Fosca, a smaller but no less lovely 11th-century church, is located next to the basilica. The early Christian architectural style is reflected in this church's basic yet exquisite design, which was constructed according to the Greek cross plan. A portico with elegant arches encircles the Church of Santa Fosca, fostering a serene and reflective ambiance. The Church of Santa Fosca and the Basilica di Santa Maria Assunta together comprise the core of Torcello's spiritual and historical legacy, and they are essential sites for any traveler to the island.

The Museo di Torcello, also known as the Torcello Museum, is another noteworthy destination on Torcello. It is housed in the Palazzo dell'Archivio and the Palazzo del Consiglio, two historic structures close to the basilica. A collection of items in the museum chronicle the history of Torcello, from its early settlement to its downfall in later decades. In addition to medieval sculptures, ceramics, and religious relics, the exhibits feature archeological discoveries, including Roman and Byzantine antiquities. The museum offers insightful information on the island's history and its contribution to the formation of Venetian culture. For those interested in history and archaeology, the museum is a great visit, and tickets may be bought on-site.

You will also see the well-known Ponte del Diavolo, often known as Devil's Bridge, a little stone bridge that crosses one of the island's waterways while exploring Torcello. This bridge is unusual since it lacks railings and parapets, which gives it a unique and enigmatic look. Local stories are associated with the moniker "Devil's Bridge," which enhances the island's allure and ageless quality. It serves as a reminder of Torcello's rich mythology and is a popular location for photos.

The island of Torcello is also known for its breathtaking natural beauty. Torcello is distinguished by its vast areas, verdant vegetation, and peaceful canals, in contrast to Venice's busy streets. The island's serene ambiance makes it the perfect spot for a contemplative moment or a leisurely stroll. You will come across meadows, gardens, and vineyards that capture the essence of Torcello's pastoral landscape as you explore the island. Visitors can interact with the lagoon's natural and historical character in Torcello, which offers a refreshing contrast to Venice's bustling tourist districts.

There are a few restaurants on Torcello that serve delectable Venetian food in a calm atmosphere for people who want to eat there. Among the most well-known is Locanda Cipriani, a historic eatery and hotel that has played host to many renowned people, including Ernest Hemingway. The restaurant's outdoor terrace offers a charming eating experience, and its traditional dishes are prepared with local, fresh ingredients. A great dining experience at Locanda Cipriani enhances the allure of a trip to Torcello.

Consider taking a guided tour that includes transportation and an informed guide who can share their knowledge of Torcello's history, landmarks, and stories if you want to get the most out of your trip. You can visit several locations in a single day because many tours also stop at other neighboring islands, such Murano and Burano. These tours can be scheduled directly with local operators or online through a number of travel agencies.

CHAPTER 5

THE VENTIAN CULTURE

Etiquette and Customs in the Area

With its distinct topography, extensive history, and lively culture, Venice is a city unlike any other. To properly enjoy the Venetian way of life and make sure that your encounters with residents are civil and pleasurable, it is imperative that visitors have a thorough awareness of local customs and etiquette. You can develop a stronger bond with the city and its residents by adhering to the traditions and legacy that the Venetians are so proud of. Despite being a popular tourist destination, Venice remains a vibrant city with its own rhythms and unspoken laws. Understanding these traditions will demonstrate your appreciation for the local way of life while also assisting you in blending in.

The tempo of Venetian life is among its most significant features. Venice's way of life is slower and more laid-back than that of many contemporary cities. This is partially because of its unusual design, which forgoes bicycles and cars in favor of foot or boat transit. Because the city's islands are connected by bridges and winding lanes, Venetians are used to walking everywhere. Accepting this slower pace and taking the time to appreciate the beauty of your surroundings is crucial for visitors. Wandering, exploring, and finding hidden corners are what make Venice so charming; hurrying around the city or attempting to follow a strict timetable might ruin the experience.

Being aware of your surroundings and thoughtful of others is crucial when strolling through Venice. Particularly during the busiest travel seasons, the city's streets and bridges can get congested and small. Because they are accustomed to using these areas well, Venetians value it when guests follow suit. To prevent obstructing foot traffic, move to the side if you need to pause for a picture, to consult a map, or to take in the scenery. In a similar vein, try to stay to one side of bridges so that others can pass. These modest acts of thoughtfulness go a long way toward demonstrating respect for the local way of life.

Recognizing the significance of the canals is another essential component of Venetian etiquette. The canals serve as roadways for trade and transit, making them more than just a beautiful aspect of the city. Private boats, vaporettos (water buses), and gondolas all use the same waterways and each plays a unique part in city life. Respecting the canals and the people who utilize them is crucial for tourists. Steer clear of tossing anything into the water as this harms the lagoon's fragile ecology and adds to pollution. Be considerate of fellow passengers and obey the directions of the boat operators when riding in a vaporetto or gondola. Although gondola rides are a classic and beautiful way to see Venice, the gondoliers take great pleasure in their work and want their customers to treat them with respect.

Knowing the habits of the locals can also improve your dining experience in Venice. Meals have a significant role in social and familial life, and Venetians take their cuisine very seriously. It is usual to say "buongiorno" (good morning) or "buonasera" (good evening) to the staff when you first visit a restaurant. Rushing through your lunch when seated at a table is considered rude. Meals are frequently unhurried affairs, and Venetians place equal significance on the dining experience as they do on the cuisine. Avoid asking for the check until you are ready to go because it is not normal for the staff to bring it without your request. Instead, take your time and enjoy the flavors and atmosphere.

Knowing that Venetian cuisine has a strong connection to the history and geography of the city is useful when placing food orders. Venice's location in the lagoon is reflected in the abundance of seafood used in many of its recipes. Local specialties that are worth tasting include risotto al nero di seppia (squid ink risotto) and sarde in saor (sweet and sour sardines). Cicchetti, which are small dishes of food akin to tapas that are usually served in bacari, or traditional wine bars, are another custom that Venetians follow. Because there is frequently a shortage of seating, it is normal to eat and drink while standing at the counter when visiting a bacaro. A glass of wine or a spritz, a well-liked aperitif made with prosecco, Aperol or Campari, and soda water, is frequently served with cicchetti by Venetians.

Another topic that tourists frequently ask about in Venice is tipping. Tipping is not customary in Italy, unlike in certain other nations, because service fees are typically covered by the bill. However, as a token of gratitude for excellent service, it is customary to leave a little change. For instance, it's considered courteous to leave a few cents on the table or round up the bill to the closest euro. Although not required, a tip of 5–10% is recommended in more premium eateries.

Venetians are renowned for their pride in their city and strong sense of community. Respecting the customs and culture of the place you are visiting is crucial. Learning a few simple Italian words and expressions, like "grazie" (thank you), "per favore" (please), and "scusi" (pardon me), is one approach to achieve this. Attempting to communicate in Italian is a sign of respect and is frequently appreciated, even if many Venetians understand English. Although most Venetians are warm and inviting, they also respect their own space and solitude. Avoid being too loud or obtrusive when engaging with locals; instead, be kind and considerate.

Being aware of the particular difficulties and weaknesses of the city is another crucial component of Venetian etiquette. Rising sea levels, pollution, and the effects of mass tourism pose a continual threat to Venice's ancient structures, canals, and lagoon, making it a delicate city. Observing sustainable tourism practices as a guest can help preserve Venice. To protect historic sites, refrain from littering, use reusable water bottles rather than single-use plastic ones, and stick to prescribed routes. Dress modestly and abide by any set guidelines, such as not snapping pictures or talking loudly, when you visit churches and other cultural sites.

Another way to improve your Venice shopping experience is to be aware of local customs. Handmade masks, Burano lace, and Murano glass are among the city's well-known artisanal crafts. It is crucial to support regional craftspeople and steer clear of mass-produced knockoffs while buying these products. You may spot true Venetian craftsmanship by looking for the certificates of authenticity that many stores show for their goods. Unless you are buying several products, in which case a slight discount might be given, it is advisable to accept the advertised price because haggling is uncommon in Venice.

It's critical to keep in mind that Venice is home to its citizens as well as a popular tourist attraction. The city and its way of life are greatly impacted by the millions of tourists that come here each year. You can demonstrate your respect for the locals as a guest by being aware of your conduct and refraining from acts that interfere with day-to-day activities. Sitting on steps or bridges, for instance, might obstruct traffic and cause annoyance for nearby residents. In a same vein, avoid feeding pigeons in St. Mark's Square as this leads to overcrowding and deteriorates the old structures.

Traditions and Festivals in Venice

In addition to its canals, architecture, and artwork, Venice is well-known for its lively festivals and rich customs that date back hundreds of years. Deeply ingrained in the history, culture, and religious beliefs of the city, these celebrations and customs still have a significant impact on Venetians' daily life.

Attending these events gives tourists a special chance to experience Venice's essence and see the city at its liveliest and most vibrant. Every festival has an own personality that blends aspects of community, history, art, and music, and both locals and tourists enjoy them with tremendous fervor. You can better appreciate the richness of Venetian culture and the pride its people have in maintaining their legacy by being aware of the significance of these celebrations and customs.

The Carnevale di Venezia, or Venice Carnival, is one of the city's most well-known and recognizable celebrations. Celebrated with elaborate costumes, masks, parades, and parties, this world-famous celebration occurs in the weeks preceding Lent. Before the serious time of Lent, Venetians used to celebrate and have fun during the 12th century, which is when the Venice Carnival got its start. People traveled from all across Europe to attend the carnival, which gained notoriety for its lavish festivities over the ages. A major component of the Venice Carnival, masks were first employed to conceal identities and social standing, fostering an environment of equality and liberation. Today, St. Mark's Square serves as the primary venue for many of the carnival's festivities, which include grand balls, street performances, and processions. From traditional designs to contemporary interpretations, the costumes and masks showcase the artistry and ingenuity of the artists. One of the city's most memorable events is the Venice Carnival, which is a celebration of art, history, and creativity. The July celebration of the Feast of the Redeemer, or Festa del Redentore, is another significant Venetian custom. The origins of this festival can be traced back to the 16th century, when a horrific plague outbreak hit Venice. In 1576, if the city was freed from the plague, the Venetian Senate promised to construct a church honoring Christ the Redeemer. The Festa del Redentore was created as a method to express gratitude once the plague ended, and the Church of the Redentore was built on the island of Giudecca. The festival's most famous feature is its amazing fireworks display, which lights up the night sky over the lagoon. It starts with a religious procession and a special mass in the church. In honor of the occasion, Venetians deck out their boats and get together for a spectacular supper on the water with loved ones. The endurance and faith of the Venetian people are reflected in the Festa del Redentore, a time of joy and thankfulness.

Another well-liked Venetian custom that occurs in September is the Regata Storica, often known as the Historical Regatta. A series of rowing competitions on the Grand Canal are part of this celebration of Venice's maritime heritage. The historical procession, which recreates the splendor of Venice's past with ornately adorned boats and gondolas staffed by rowers dressed in traditional garb, is the highlight of the Regata Storica. Competitive races, such as the renowned gondolini race, where talented rowers vie for victory, take place after the procession. In addition to being an exciting sight, the Regata Storica serves as a reminder of the city's strong ties to the sea and its maritime heritage. Visitors can experience the thrill of a centuries-old rivalry while also witnessing the talent and commitment of Venetian rowers.

Another significant Venetian celebration that stretches back to the Venetian Republic is the Festa della Sensa, also known as the Feast of the Ascension. This celebration honors Venice's nautical might and her longstanding bond with the sea. The symbolic "Marriage of the Sea" event, which is the centerpiece of the Festa della Sensa, is when the mayor of Venice, speaking on behalf of the city, tosses a gold ring into the ocean to reestablish Venice's connection to the sea. Venice used this custom, which dates back to the tenth century, to demonstrate its control over the Adriatic. The festival is a celebration of Venice's history and identity that also features religious rituals, cultural festivities, and a regatta.

Venice hosts several customs and celebrations that showcase the city's distinct culture in addition to these significant festivals. For instance, the Feast of St. Mark, also known as the Festa di San Marco, is observed on April 25th in honor of the patron saint of Venice. Venetians honor St. Mark on this day with parades, cultural festivals, and religious services held at St. Mark's Basilica. Because it is customary for males to present ladies they love with a red rose, called a "bocolo," it is also a day to show love and affection. Faith, love, and Venetian pride are all celebrated at the Festa di San Marco.

The Vogalonga, a non-competitive rowing competition held in May, is another beloved custom. In order to increase awareness of the effects of motorized boats on the lagoon and to encourage the preservation of Venice's rowing traditions, the Vogalonga was founded in the 1970s. In a vibrant and joyous setting, participants row a 30-kilometer course that winds through the city's canals and the nearby islands. All skill levels of rowers are welcome to participate in the Vogalonga, which honors Venice's ties to the water and its dedication to sustainability.

Venice is also well-known for its cultural and artistic events, like the Venice Film Festival and the Venice Biennale. One of the world's most prominent exhibitions of contemporary art, the Venice Biennale is held every two years. In addition to events devoted to architecture, dance, music, and theater, it showcases artwork created by artists from all over the world. The oldest film festival in the world, the Venice Film Festival takes place on the Lido every year and draws actors, directors, and moviegoers from all over the world. These gatherings demonstrate Venice's status as a major hub for art and culture worldwide as well as the city's ongoing inventiveness and inventiveness.

To sum up, Venice's celebrations and customs provide witness to her illustrious past, lively culture, and resilient nature. These festivities, which range from the seriousness of the Festa del Redentore to the grandeur of the Venice Carnival, give visitors an insight into the essence of Venetian life and leave them with life-changing memories. Visitors can connect with the city's legacy, enjoy its artistic and cultural accomplishments, and experience the excitement and pride of its residents by taking part in these events. Venice's customs and festivals are more than merely occasions; they serve as reminders of the city's special position in the world and as representations of its identity.

Language Advice for Travelers

Knowing a few essential words and phrases can help you better connect with the locals and make the most of your trip to Venice. Although many Venetians, particularly those employed in the tourism sector, speak English, it is respectful to try to acquire and use a few Italian terms and phrases as it can improve the quality of your interactions. Additionally, it demonstrates your admiration for and willingness to interact more deeply with the local culture. Many residents, especially those in the older generations, still speak the Venetian dialect, also referred to as "Venetian" or "Veneto," even though Italian is the main language spoken in the city. While it is not required of visitors to speak Venetian, knowing a few Italian words and the fundamentals of communication might help your trip go more smoothly and enjoyably.

Being courteous is highly regarded in Italian, which is one of the most crucial things to keep in mind when speaking the language. "Please," "thank you," and "excuse me" are simple yet effective ways to make a good impression. For instance, the phrase "per favore," which translates to "please," is used when requesting anything. Meaning "thank you," "grazie" is one of the most often used words you may encounter when traveling. You can say "prego," which translates to "you're welcome," in response to "grazie." These minor acts of civility are valued and can improve your relationships with locals.
Until about lunchtime, "buongiorno," or "good morning," is the standard way to greet someone. Then you can use "buonasera," which means "good evening." "Ciao" is a

friendly and informal way to say both "hello" and "goodbye" if you are not sure what time of day it is or if you want to use a more general greeting. However, remember that "ciao" is usually used among friends and acquaintances, so it is better to use "buongiorno" or "buonasera" when addressing someone you do not know well, like a waiter or store owner. To say "goodbye" in a more formal manner, use "arrivederci," which translates to "goodbye."

When requesting assistance or directions, it is considered polite to start your question with "scusi," which translates to "excuse me." For instance, if you are trying to find a specific place, you could say, "Scusi, dov'è...?" which translates to "Excuse me, where is...?" Adding "per favore" at the end of your question makes it even more polite. Venetians are generally amiable and eager to assist, especially if you try to speak their language. For example, "Scusi, dov'è Piazza San Marco, per favore?" means "Excuse me, where is St. Mark's Square, please?"

There are a few expressions that can be especially helpful while ordering meals or dining in a restaurant. When you walk into a restaurant, you should say "buongiorno" or "buonasera" to the staff. If you want a table, you can say "Un tavolo per due, per favore," which translates to "A table for two, please." If you are ready to place your order, you can say "Vorrei..." followed by the name of the dish or drink you want. Additionally, when you are looking at the menu, you might want to ask for recommendations by saying "Cosa mi consiglia?" which translates to "What do you recommend?"

When you are done eating and ready to pay, you might say "Il conto, per favore," which translates to "The bill, please," to request the check. For instance, "Vorrei una pizza margherita" means "I would like a margherita pizza."

Knowing a few phrases can help you enjoy your shopping experience in Venice, whether you're in a market, boutique, or souvenir shop. Venetians value patience and politeness, so taking the time to use these phrases can make your shopping experience more enjoyable. For example, if you want to ask how much something costs, you can say "Quanto costa?" which means "How much does it cost?" If you decide to buy something, you can say "Lo prendo," which means "I'll take it." If you are browsing and do not need assistance, you can politely say "Sto solo guardando," which means "I'm just looking."

Another area where knowing a few Italian phrases can be useful is in transportation. It may be necessary to confirm your stop or ask for directions if you are riding the vaporetto, Venice's public water bus. "Qual è la fermata per…?" means "Which is the stop for…?" If you need to purchase a ticket, you can say "Un biglietto per il vaporetto, per favore," which means "A ticket for the vaporetto, please." If you are unclear of the schedule, you can ask, "A che ora parte il vaporetto?" which means "What time does the vaporetto leave?"

Knowing a few terms and expressions unique to Venice is also beneficial, in addition to these useful ones. For instance, most squares in the city are called "campo" (Venetian for "square" or "plaza") rather than "piazza" (Late Italian). "Rio" means a little canal, while "calle" means a narrow street. You can read maps and get around the city more efficiently if you know these terminology. Additionally, the word "bacaro" is used by Venetians to describe a classic wine bar where cicchetti, or tiny plates of food, are served. You can improve your experience and feel more a part of the place by being familiar with this local lingo.

Being aware of some cultural communication differences is beneficial, even though knowing a few Italian phrases is crucial. Venetians and other Italians have a propensity for being expressive and emphasizing their statements with gestures. Additionally, they respect direct eye contact since it is interpreted as an indication of sincerity and interest. Try to keep your communication style open and warm when interacting with locals, and don't be scared to utilize gestures to express yourself. Your attempt to communicate, despite your imperfect Italian, will be valued.

In conclusion, you can significantly improve your travel experience by knowing a few essential Italian phrases and comprehending the fundamentals of Venetian communication. These linguistic guidelines will help you connect with the people and make your interactions more enjoyable, whether you're ordering meals, greeting them, or traversing the city and asking for directions. Venetians value tourists who try to participate in their customs since they are proud of their language and heritage. You can establish deep connections and have a greater understanding of Venice's beauty and charm by utilizing these expressions and demonstrating respect for the local way of life.

CHAPTER 6

VENICE'S CUISINE AND DRINKS

Things to Try in Venetian Cuisine

The distinctive topography, history, and culture of Venice are all reflected in its food. Venice, surrounded by water and shaped by centuries of trade with far-off places, has a unique culinary legacy that is firmly anchored in its nautical history. In addition to sating hunger, Venice's cuisine offers an opportunity to enjoy the smells, scents, and customs that have been preserved throughout the years. There are several foods and culinary experiences that visitors should not miss, and sampling Venetian cuisine is a crucial element of comprehending the city's identity. Venetian food offers a vast array of flavors to suit every palate, from modest morsels consumed in classic wine bars to seafood specialties and decadent desserts.

Cicchetti, which are little plates or appetizers that are frequently likened to Spanish tapas, are among the most recognizable features of Venetian cuisine. Cicchetti are a common option for a fast bite or informal dinner when touring the city, and they are usually served in bacari, which are classic Venetian wine taverns. Traditionally served with a glass of wine or a spritz—a traditional Venetian aperitif consisting of prosecco, Aperol or Campari, and soda water—these little plates are meant to be shared. Cheeses, veggies, cured meats, and seafood are just a few of the many flavors and components that can be added to spaghetti. Crostini topped with marinated anchovies, polpette (meatballs), and baccalà mantecato (creamed salt cod) are typical cicchetti examples. Every bacaro has its own specialties, and sampling the food at various restaurants is part of the excitement. In addition to being tasty, clicchetti are a wonderful way to experience the social aspect of Venetian dining, as both locals and tourists congregate in these welcoming wine bars to savor delectable cuisine and stimulating conversation.

Because of the city's location in the lagoon and its long history as a nautical power, seafood is a major component of Venetian cuisine. Sarde in saor, a typical Middle Ages sardine preparation, is one of Venice's most well-known seafood dishes. Sarde in saor is made with fried sardines marinated in a vinegar, onion, pine nut, and raisins mixture. Originally used to preserve fish for long trips, this blend of sweet and sour flavors is a hallmark of Venetian cooking. Sarde in saor is a popular dish nowadays, frequently served as an appetizer or as a component of a selection of cicchetti. It is a must-try for anybody traveling to Venice because of its distinctive flavor profile and historical significance.

Risotto al nero di seppia, or squid ink risotto, is another classic seafood dish. This meal has a deep, salty flavor and a striking appearance since the rice is cooked in a rich, black sauce made from cuttlefish ink. A classic example of how Venetian cooking uses the resources found in the lagoon to create visually attractive and wonderfully tasty dishes is risotto al nero di seppia. This meal is a favorite among seafood enthusiasts because of the risotto's creamy texture and the squid ink's umami-rich flavor. It goes well with a glass of Venetian white wine and is frequently offered as a main entrée in classic Venetian restaurants.

Venetian cuisine is well-known for its savory dishes as well as its simple yet decadent sweets. Tiramisu, a layered dessert prepared with coffee-soaked ladyfingers, mascarpone cheese, cocoa powder, and a touch of liquor, is one of the most well-known sweets connected to Venice. Despite being popular throughout Italy and the rest of the world, tiramisu is thought to have originated in the Veneto region, which makes it a suitable dessert option when dining in Venice. Rich coffee, bittersweet cocoa, and creamy mascarpone combine to make a dessert that is both elegant and comforting.

Fritole, or fritters, are another classic Venetian dish that is usually consumed during the Carnival season. Little balls of fried dough called fritole are frequently seasoned with pine nuts, raisins, and a touch of citrus zest. For an added touch of decadence, they are occasionally filled with cream or custard and sprinkled with powdered sugar. A wonderful dessert that embodies the city's joyful spirit, fritole has been a part of Venetian culinary tradition for decades. Fritole are a delectable way to sample the sweeter side of Venetian cuisine, whether they are eaten as a dessert after a meal or as a snack while walking the streets.

When dining out or browsing local markets, there are a few terms that travelers who wish to thoroughly immerse themselves in Venetian food culture may find useful to know. It is considered courteous to say "buongiorno" (good morning) or "buonasera" (good evening) to the personnel as you enter a restaurant or bacaro. When ordering cicchetti, you can just say "questo, per favore" (this one, please) while pointing to the goods you want. You might say "uno spritz, per favore" (a spritz, please) or "un bicchiere di vino bianco, per favore" (a glass of white wine, please) when placing your drink order. "Cosa mi consiglia?" (What do you recommend?) is a way to ask the staff for suggestions if you are not sure what to order. "Il conto, per favore" (The bill, please) is a way to request the check when you are prepared to pay. These short expressions can enhance your eating experience and demonstrate your respect for the local way of life.

Where to Get Food and Drink

A distinctive culinary experience that reflects the city's nautical origins and centuries of trading with far-off places, Venetian food is an intriguing fusion of history, geography, and culture. In addition to providing sustenance, Venice's cuisine serves as a bridge to the city's customs and populace. Since each dish reflects the lagoon, the sea, and the active life of this unique location, tourists must try Venetian food in order to fully comprehend the city's personality. Venetian cuisine is a feast for the senses, ranging from tiny, tasty morsels to rich seafood feasts and decadent sweets. To fully experience Venice's flavors, every visitor should try a few delicacies.

Cicchetti, which are little plates or appetizers that are frequently likened to Spanish tapas, are among the most recognizable features of Venetian cuisine. A staple of Venetian cuisine, cicchetti are usually consumed in bacari, which are classic wine taverns located all across the city. Typically served with a glass of wine or a spritz—a traditional Venetian aperitif made with prosecco, Aperol or Campari, and soda water—these little bites are meant to be shared. Cicchetti are a great way to introduce people to Venetian cuisine because they can be made with a wide range of ingredients and flavors. Crostini covered with baccalà mantecato, a creamy spread made with salt cod, olive oil, and garlic, is among the most well-liked cicchetti. A Venetian staple, this dish is adored for its delicate flavor and silky texture. Other popular cicchetti include marinated anchovies, which are sometimes served with a sprinkling of parsley and a drop of olive oil, and polpette, which are tiny meatballs prepared from beef, pork, or even fish. Cicchetti also incorporates vegetables; grilled eggplant, zucchini, and artichokes are common menu items. Every bacaro has its own specialties, and sampling the food at various businesses is part of the excitement of eating cicchetti. This custom of sharing small plates in a laid-back, communal setting is a great way to get a taste of Venice's delicacies and experience the local way of life.

Because of the city's location in the lagoon and its long history as a nautical power, seafood is central to Venetian cuisine. Sarde in saor, a typical Middle Ages sardine preparation, is one of Venice's most well-known seafood dishes. Fresh sardines are marinated in a mixture of vinegar, onions, raisins, and pine nuts before being fried to make sarde in saor. Originally used to preserve fish for long trips, this blend of sweet and sour flavors is a hallmark of Venetian cooking. Because of its distinct flavor profile and historical significance, the dish is frequently served as an appetizer or as part of a cicchetti selection. A complex and filling dish is produced by balancing the vinegar's acidity and the sardines' richness with the sweetness of the raisins and the crunch of the pine nuts. Anyone visiting Venice should sample Sarde in Saor, which gives a taste of the city's gastronomic history and its relationship to the sea.

Risotto al nero di seppia, or squid ink risotto, is another classic seafood dish. This meal has a deep, salty flavor and a striking appearance since the rice is cooked in a rich, black sauce made from cuttlefish ink. A classic example of how Venetian cooking uses the resources found in the lagoon to create visually attractive and wonderfully tasty dishes is risotto al nero di seppia. This meal is a favorite among seafood enthusiasts because of the risotto's creamy texture and the squid ink's umami-rich flavor. It goes well with a glass of Venetian white wine and is frequently offered as a main entrée in classic Venetian restaurants. In addition to being delicious, the dish showcases the inventiveness and resourcefulness of Venetian chefs, who have long used the abundance of the sea to produce their culinary creations.

Venetian cuisine is well-known for its savory dishes as well as its simple yet decadent sweets. Tiramisu, a layered dessert prepared with coffee-soaked ladyfingers, mascarpone cheese, cocoa powder, and a touch of liquor, is one of the most well-known sweets connected to Venice. Despite being popular throughout Italy and the rest of the world, tiramisu is thought to have originated in the Veneto region, which makes it a suitable dessert option when dining in Venice. Rich coffee, bittersweet cocoa, and creamy mascarpone combine to make a dessert that is both elegant and comforting. Tiramisu's delicate, airy texture makes it the ideal way to finish a meal, and it's frequently served in individual portions.

Fritole, or fritters, are another classic Venetian dish that is usually consumed during the Carnival season. Little balls of fried dough called fritole are frequently seasoned with pine nuts, raisins, and a touch of citrus zest. For an added touch of decadence, they are occasionally filled with cream or custard and sprinkled with powdered sugar. A wonderful dessert that embodies the city's joyful spirit, fritole has been a part of Venetian culinary tradition for decades. Fritole are a delectable way to sample the sweeter side of Venetian cuisine, whether they are eaten as a dessert after a meal or as a snack while walking the streets.

When dining out or browsing local markets, there are a few terms that travelers who wish to thoroughly immerse themselves in Venetian food culture may find useful to know. It is considered courteous to say "buongiorno" (good morning) or "buonasera" (good evening) to the personnel as you enter a restaurant or bacaro. When ordering cicchetti, you can just say "questo, per favore" (this one, please) while pointing to the goods you want. You might say "uno spritz, per favore" (a spritz, please) or "un bicchiere di vino bianco, per favore" (a glass of white wine, please) when placing your drink order. "Cosa mi consiglia?" (What do you recommend?) is a way to ask the staff for suggestions if you are not sure what to order. "Il conto, per favore" (The bill, please) is a way to request the check when you are prepared to pay. These short expressions can enhance your eating experience and demonstrate your respect for the local way of life.

Experiences with Food

Eating is only one aspect of Venetian cuisine; another is using it to experience Venice's history, culture, and customs. One of the most fulfilling ways for visitors to engage with Venice is to immerse themselves in its culinary culture. Beyond just going to restaurants and trying out local cuisine, you can get a deeper understanding of Venetian culinary culture by taking part in interactive activities and seeing the areas where people congregate and shop. Visiting the Rialto Market and enrolling in a Venetian cooking lesson are two of the most rewarding culinary adventures in Venice. Through these events, tourists can become active participants in the city's culinary traditions rather than only passive observers. Anyone who enjoys food and culture will find them to be unforgettable experiences as they offer a deeper understanding of the ingredients, methods, and tales that go into Venetian cuisine.

One of the greatest methods to discover the distinctive culinary customs of Venice is to enroll in a cooking class. Because Venice was a significant commerce hub throughout the

Venetian Republic, it has a long history of combining flavors and ingredients from around the globe. Taking a cooking class gives you the opportunity to learn how to make classic Venetian food while also learning about the culture and history that influenced it. Local chefs or home cooks who are enthusiastic about conserving and promoting their culinary history frequently teach these sessions. They offer a friendly and engaging setting where people may practice skills, ask questions, and take pleasure in making meals from scratch.

Learning about the main components used in regional cuisine may be the first topic covered in a normal Venetian cooking session. These frequently consist of seasonal vegetables, fresh seafood from the lagoon, and basic foods like rice and polenta. The instructor may go over the origins of these ingredients and their significance in Venetian cooking. For instance, Venice's location in the lagoon means that seafood is a major component of its cuisine. Dishes like risotto al nero di seppia (squid ink risotto) and sarde in saor (sweet and sour sardines) highlight the city's dependence on the sea. The usage of spices like cloves, nutmeg, and cinnamon—which were brought to Venetian cuisine through commerce with the East—may also be covered for participants. These spices are still employed in some traditional dishes.

Making a multi-course dinner, which may include an appetizer, a main dish, and a dessert, is usually the hands-on component of the lesson. For instance, attendees can learn how to prepare baccalà mantecato, a creamy spread made with salt fish that is frequently served as an appetizer on crostini. After that, they can proceed to prepare a seafood risotto, learning how to balance the tastes and achieve the ideal creamy texture. They may make tiramisu, a traditional Venetian dessert consisting of layers of mascarpone cheese, cocoa powder, and ladyfingers steeped in coffee, for dessert. Throughout the lesson, the instructor may give stories about the meals' origins and cultural significance in Venice, along with helpful hints for handling the materials.

The ability to sit down and savor the cooked food is one of the best aspects of a cooking class. This is frequently carried out in a group environment where members can exchange their work and consider what they have discovered. It's an opportunity to enjoy Venice's flavors more intimately and personally while knowing that you helped create them. In order to enable students to replicate the dishes and share their Venetian experience with friends and family, many culinary workshops also provide them recipes to follow at home.

Exploring the Rialto Market, one of the liveliest and most historic locations in Venice, is another must-do culinary adventure. This market, which is close to the famous Rialto Bridge, has long been a center of daily life and business in Venice. It provides a window into the rhythms of Venetian life and is a place where locals go to purchase fresh produce, seafood, and other goods. The Rialto Market offers visitors the chance to experience the sights, sounds, and scents of a typical market as well as the origins of the products that make up Venetian cuisine.

The Pescheria, or fish market, and the Erberia, or produce market, are the two primary divisions of the Rialto Market. With stands brimming with fresh seafood from the lagoon and beyond, the Pescheria is a sensory feast. Everything from clams and mussels to squid, shrimp, and even fish can be found here. The seafood is presented with care and attention to detail, and the vendors take great delight in the caliber of their offerings. As you go through the fish market, you may hear the vendors shouting to customers, giving their daily catch and cooking advice. Venice's strong ties to the water and its dependence on the lagoon for food are demonstrated by the diversity and freshness of its seafood.

Stalls brimming with vibrant fruits and vegetables make up the equally spectacular Erberia, or produce market. You may see artichokes from the nearby island of Sant'Erasmo, which are valued for their delicate flavor and sensitive texture, depending on the season. Other seasonal delights could be asparagus, figs, or radicchio. Learn about the key ingredients used in Venetian cookery and observe how they vary with the seasons at the produce market. It's a great chance to learn about the local food culture because many of the vendors are willing to answer questions and share their experience.

For visitors, the Rialto Market offers more than simply shopping; it's an opportunity to take in the vibrancy and ambience of a location that has long been central to Venetian culture. It's an opportunity to see how vendors and customers interact, to witness the attention to detail that goes into choosing the finest products, and to recognize the significance of food in Venetian daily life. Additionally, the market is an excellent place to buy locally produced olive oil, dried pasta, spices, and other mementos or items to take home.

Knowing a few essential Italian phrases might help you get the most out of your trip to the Rialto Market. "Quanto costa?" (How much does it cost?) is one way to inquire about the price of something. You may say "Lo prendo" (I'll take it) if you choose to purchase something. "Sto solo guardando" (I'm just looking) is a courteous way to express that you are merely perusing. These short words can improve the quality of your relationships with the suppliers and express gratitude for their efforts.

CHAPTER 7

NAVIGATING VENICE

Strolling about Venice

In Venice, strolling around the city is one of the most fulfilling and engaging experiences. Venice is a pedestrian-only city without vehicles, buses, or bicycles, in contrast to most other places in the globe. The streets have a distinctive urban structure that resembles a maze since they are winding, small, and frequently connected by bridges that span the canals. For visitors, strolling in Venice is not only a useful mode of transportation but also a crucial component of taking in the beauty, charm, and history of the city. Whether it's a centuries-old church, a secret courtyard, or a peaceful canal, there's something new around every curve. However, Venice's streets are notoriously complex, making it difficult to navigate, especially for first-time tourists. Walking in Venice may become a once-in-a-lifetime experience with a little planning and some useful advice.

When it comes to walking in Venice, one of the first things to grasp is that the city is composed of more than 100 tiny islands that are connected by bridges. Unlike in many contemporary towns, the streets, or "calli" as they are known in Venetian, are frequently winding and tiny. Rather, they veer in unpredictable directions, perhaps leading to dead ends or opening onto canals without a bridge in sight. This can make getting lost easier, but it's not always a negative thing in Venice. Actually, a lot of tourists think that one of the best ways to find the city's hidden gems is to just roam around it. To avoid annoyance and maximize your time, it is still beneficial to have a basic awareness of how to get around the city.

Following the signs is one of the most crucial pieces of advice for navigating Venice. Major sites including "San Marco" (St. Mark's Square), "Rialto" (the Rialto Bridge), and "Ferrovia" (the rail station) are marked with yellow signage with black text around the city. These signs are a dependable method of getting your bearings and are typically displayed on the sides of buildings at crossroads. Look for these signs and follow them if you are attempting to get to a specific location. Though the signs are meant to orient pedestrians along the main thoroughfares, bear in mind that they might not always take you in the most direct direction. You might need to use a map or a navigation software if you would rather travel a less traveled or more picturesque route.

Learn some fundamental Venetian phrases so you can better comprehend the city's layout. This is another helpful advice. For instance, "campiello" is a smaller square, whereas "campo" is a square or plaza. A "fondamenta" is a street that runs alongside a canal, whereas "calle" is the name for a street. "Rio" refers to a little waterway, while "ponte" indicates bridge. It may be simpler to understand signs and maps and to request directions if necessary if you know these phrases. It is courteous to begin with "Scusi" (Excuse me) before posing your query if you do need assistance. Saying "Scusi, dov'è

Piazza San Marco?" (Pardon me, where is St. Mark's Square?) is one example.

Wearing comfy shoes is essential when strolling about Venice. You will probably be walking a lot and climbing a lot of bridges because the city's streets are made of stone. Shoes with thin soles or high heels are not advised since they might make walking on uneven ground uncomfortable and sometimes dangerous. Wearing strong, supportive shoes that can withstand the cobblestones and the odd puddle is preferable. When visiting Venice, it is advisable to pack waterproof shoes or boots because the city is prone to flooding, particularly during the "acqua alta" season of high tide.

The chance to stroll along Venice's many picturesque streets is one of the pleasures of wandering there. Even if the city's major tourist destinations, such as St. Mark's Square and the Rialto Bridge, are unquestionably worthwhile, some of the most stunning and serene spots are hidden away. The Dorsoduro neighborhood, for instance, is renowned for its serene alleys, quaint canals, and breathtaking vistas of the Grand Canal. Admire stunning views of the island of Giudecca and the Giudecca Canal from the Zattere promenade, which stretches along Dorsoduro's southern side. At sunset, when the light bounces off the river and the buildings turn golden, this path is particularly beautiful.

The Fondamenta della Misericordia in the Cannaregio area is another beautiful strolling path. You can stop for a glass of wine and some cicchetti (Venetian tapas) at a number of classic bacari (wine bars) in this less congested region of Venice than the more central areas. This neighborhood has a laid-back, genuine vibe with canals surrounded with vibrant buildings. You may explore the historic Jewish Ghetto, one of the oldest in Europe, while strolling through Cannaregio. It provides an intriguing look into Venice's cosmopolitan past.

A stroll along the Riva degli Schiavoni is essential for anyone wishing to take in Venice's splendor. This broad waterfront promenade, which stretches from St. Mark's Square to the Arsenale, provides breathtaking views of the lagoon as well as the islands of Giudecca and San Giorgio Maggiore. You will visit famous sites like the Church of San Zaccaria and the Bridge of Sighs along the route. Although there may be a lot of tourists on this path, the scenery and sense of history make it worthwhile.

Consider visiting the island of Giudecca if you want a more peaceful experience. This island provides a tranquil getaway from the bustle of Venice and is only a short vaporetto (water bus) journey from the city center. You may take in expansive views of the Venetian skyline while strolling along Giudecca's coastline, which includes the bell tower of the Campanile and the domes of St. Mark's Basilica. In addition, the island has antique churches, lovely gardens, and neighborhood eateries where you can eat in peace.

Spend some time admiring the little things that give Venice its distinct character as you stroll about it. Admire the buildings' elaborate façade, many of which are from the Baroque and

Renaissance eras. Take note of the windowsills' vibrant flowers and the bridges' elaborate ironwork. Take in the city's sounds, from the distant ringing of church bells to the sound of the river rushing against the canals. Walking in Venice is about more than just going from one location to another; it's about taking in the ambiance and finding hidden beauty everywhere you look.

Options for Public Transportation

There is nothing like public transportation in Venice. Because the city is located on a system of canals and the historic center is completely devoid of automobiles, busses, or trains, walking and water-based transit are the only ways to get around. To effectively navigate the city and take in its distinct beauty, visitors must be aware of Venice's public transportation alternatives. The vaporetto, or water bus, and water taxis, or private motorboats, are Venice's two primary modes of public transportation. Every choice has a distinct function, and using them appropriately can greatly improve the efficiency and enjoyment of your visit. For longer distances, such across islands or getting to your lodging with bags, public transportation is required, even if walking is frequently the greatest way to discover Venice's winding lanes and secret nooks. You can maximize your time in Venice and prevent needless confusion by becoming knowledgeable about the vaporetto routes, ticketing system, and function of water taxis.

The mainstay of Venice's public transportation network is the vaporetto. Vaporettos are big powered boats that operate similarly to buses and have set routes and schedules. They are run by ACTV, the local public transportation provider. They are the most practical and reasonably priced means of getting around Venice and the nearby islands of Lido, Murano, and Burano. Most areas of the city are easily accessible thanks to the vaporetto network, which spans the Grand Canal, the surrounding canals, and the lagoon. The vaporetto is a necessary form of transportation for travelers, particularly if they intend to visit the islands or are lodging in a hotel or apartment remote from the major attractions.

You must buy a ticket or travel pass in order to utilize the vaporetto. Tickets are available for purchase online via the ACTV website or app, at ticket offices, or at self-service kiosks at significant vaporetto stops. The price of one ticket is €9.50, and it is good for 75 minutes after it is validated. This implies that you can switch between vaporetto lines throughout that time period using the same ticket. However, buying a trip card is more cost-effective for visitors who intend to utilize the vaporetto several times while they are there. With a 1-day pass starting at €25, ACTV offers passes for 1, 2, 3, or 7 days. During the validity period, these permits provide unrestricted travel on all ACTV buses and vaporettos (on the mainland). Before boarding, you must tap your ticket or pass on the electronic reader at the vaporetto stop to confirm it. It's crucial to keep in mind that failing to confirm your ticket could result in a fine.

Once you know the fundamentals, navigating the vaporetto routes is rather simple because they are numbered and color-coded. Line 1, which follows the Grand Canal and makes stops at significant sights such Piazzale Roma (the main bus terminal), the train station (Santa Lucia), Rialto Bridge, and St. Mark's Square, is the most popular tourist route. Line 1 is the best option for sightseeing because it is a slower route with lots of stops. Although it makes fewer stops, Line 2 is a quicker option if you're in a rush and still serves the Grand Canal. Additional crucial routes are Line 12, which goes to Burano and Torcello, and Line 3, which links Venice and Murano. Additionally, there are routes to Giudecca, a more sedate residential neighborhood with breathtaking city views, and the Lido, an island famous for its beaches. Before your journey, it is an excellent idea to familiarize yourself with the routes you will probably take by studying a vaporetto map.

The vaporetto is inexpensive and practical, but it can get crowded, particularly during rush hours and popular travel seasons. Try to travel early in the morning or late at night to avoid the throng. Be ready for a crowded environment and the risk of standing during your trip if you are carrying luggage. It's also important to note that some vaporettos include outside dining spaces with breathtaking city and canal views. Sit outside and take in the surroundings while you're traveling if you can.

In contrast, water taxis are a more opulent and exclusive mode of transportation in Venice. These streamlined motorboats are a fantastic choice in some circumstances because they are quicker and more straightforward than vaporettos. A water taxi, for instance, can transport you straight to your hotel or destination without requiring you to negotiate congested vaporettos or walk considerable distances if you are traveling in a group or have a lot of luggage. Because they provide a more individualized and comfortable experience, water taxis are also a popular option for special events like romantic getaways or airport transfers.

The cost of a water taxi might vary based on the distance, time of day, and number of passengers, but it is substantially more expensive than a vaporetto. While a shuttle from Marco Polo Airport to the city can cost €100 or more, a normal ride within the city center can cost between €40 and €70. It's a good idea to settle on the fee with the driver before you set off to avoid any surprises. Although many water taxis also take credit cards, it's a good idea to have cash on hand in case something goes wrong.

You have two options for renting a water taxi: either phone a water taxi operator to schedule a pickup, or visit one of the approved water taxi stands, which are located at important locations like Piazzale Roma, the train station, and St. Mark's Square. It is worthwhile to inquire with your lodging as some hotels additionally provide their clients with private water taxi services. A business that specialized in airport transfers, such as Consorzio Motoscafi Venezia, allows you to reserve a water taxi in advance if you are going to or from the airport.

Although they are comfortable and convenient, water taxis are not always required. Walking is frequently the greatest method to discover Venice's winding lanes and hidden gems, and for the majority of visitors, the vaporetto is adequate for traveling around the city. A water taxi, however, might be a good investment if you are pressed for time, have mobility problems, or just want to take in a more private and picturesque journey.

An understanding of a few essential Italian phrases will help you get the most out of Venice's public transportation system. For instance, "Dov'è la fermata del vaporetto?" (Where is the vaporetto stop?) might be used to inquire about its location. "Quale linea devo prendere?" (Which line should I take?) is a question you can ask to find out which line to take. You can check the pricing by asking, "Quanto costa per andare a...?" (How much does it cost to go to...?) before getting into a water taxi. These short words can improve the ease and enjoyment of your encounters with locals and transportation personnel.

Gondola Rides: A Timeless Adventure

One of Venice's most recognizable and unforgettable experiences is riding a gondola, which gives tourists an opportunity to view the city from the sea, which is its most distinctive viewpoint. Gondolas have been a representation of Venice's history, culture, and romantic charm for centuries. Although gondolas used to be the main means of transportation in the city, they are now primarily utilized for tourist and pleasure. Gondola rides are more than simply a means of transportation; they're an opportunity to take in the peace and beauty of Venice's waterways. A gondola ride is frequently one of the highlights of a visitor's trip and is considered a must-do activity for many. To get the most out of this traditional Venetian experience, it's crucial to comprehend how gondola rides operate, how to pick the best one, what to anticipate, and how much they cost.

Long, slender, and flat-bottomed, gondolas are a classic Venetian watercraft that is made especially for negotiating the shallow waters of the city's canals. In keeping with a centuries-old custom, each gondola is handcrafted and painted black. At the rear of the boat, the gondolier, who is in charge of steering the gondola, propels and directs it through the water with a single oar. Because maneuvering through the canals demands accuracy and technique, gondoliers are extremely talented. In order to be authorized to operate a gondola, they must pass stringent tests and complete extensive training. Gondoliers take tremendous pleasure in their role as representatives of Venetian culture, and many come from families with a long history of working in this field.

Because there are so many gondolas and gondoliers in the city, selecting a gondola trip can be both an exhilarating and occasionally daunting affair. Gondolas can be found at specific gondola stations, which are close to important sites including the Grand Canal, the Rialto Bridge, and St. Mark's Square. Gondolas can also be found in more sedate parts of the city, where the mood is calmer and the canals are less congested. Think about the type of experience you want while choosing a gondola ride destination. A trip around the Grand Canal or close to St. Mark's Square would be perfect if you want to visit well-known sites and take in the vibrant spirit of Venice. A gondola ride in a less visited region, like the Cannaregio or Dorsoduro districts, might be your best option, though, if you're looking for a more private and tranquil experience. You can discover secret waterways and see a new side of Venice by taking these more sedate paths.

It's crucial to speak with the gondolier while selecting a gondola to make sure your needs are satisfied. Many gondoliers speak simple English and are often amiable and approachable. Before the voyage starts, let the gondolier know if you have a certain route or destination in mind. For instance, you could say, "Possiamo andare in una zona tranquilla?" (Can we go to a calm area?) or "Vorrei vedere il Canal Grande" (I would want to see the Grand Canal). "Cosa mi consiglia?" (What do you recommend?) is a way to ask the gondolier for advice if you are not sure where to go. Remember that gondola trips have a set length and cost, so there may be time restrictions on the route. Despite these limitations, the majority of gondoliers are pleased to personalize the experience.

Although lengthier rides can be requested for an additional fee, a typical gondola journey lasts roughly thirty minutes. You may anticipate riding at a leisurely speed along Venice's canals as you pass by quaint bridges, old buildings, and scenic vistas. The experience may be enhanced if the gondolier shares fascinating anecdotes or facts about the city. While it's not a given and could cost extra, some gondoliers also perform traditional Venetian tunes. It is recommended to ask about a singing gondolier in advance if you are interested in having one. You can go with friends or family because gondolas can hold up to six people. A private ride for two will cost the same as a shared ride for six, though, because the pricing is the same for all passengers.

The city of Venice controls the price of gondola rides, and all gondoliers are required to charge the same prices. Currently, a half-hour gondola ride during the day costs €80, and a half-hour ride in the evening (after 7:00 PM) costs €100. Additional time is paid at €40 per 20 minutes during the day and €50 per 20 minutes in the evening if you would want to prolong the ride. The fee can be split among the passengers because these rates are for the full gondola and not per person. It's crucial to remember that these prices are set and that gondoliers are not permitted to charge more than the stated amounts. It is wise to check the cost before the trip starts, though, as some gondoliers could attempt to haggle for higher prices with visitors who are not aware of the regulations. Saying "Quanto costa?" (How much does it cost?) and making sure the gondolier gives you the official amount will accomplish this.

Although gondola rides are a fantastic experience, they are not the most cost-effective or practical means of transportation in Venice. The vaporetto (water bus) or a water taxi would be better choices if you're searching for transportation rather than entertainment. Whether you are celebrating a milestone, a romantic occasion, or just taking in the magic of Venice, gondola rides are best appreciated as a special treat. Consider taking a gondola ride in the evening or around sunset, when the city is illuminated by gentle light and the canals are more tranquil, to enhance the experience and make it even more unforgettable. A genuinely remarkable ambiance is produced by the lights' reflections on the water.

Gondola rides are a traditional Venetian activity that provide a distinctive approach to explore the city and get a sense of its culture and history. You can make sure that your gondola journey is stress-free and enjoyable by knowing how it operates, how to pick the best one, and what to anticipate. A gondola ride is an opportunity to calm down, breathe in the beauty of Venice, and make lifelong memories, whether you are drifting along the Grand Canal or discovering secret canals. This age-old custom can turn into one of your favorite parts of your trip to Venice if you prepare ahead of time and keep an open mind.

CHAPTER 8

VENICE DAY TRIPS

Exploring the Veneto Area

Verona

Often called the "City of Romeo and Juliet," Verona is one of Italy's most charming cities and a great day trip option from Venice. Verona is a city rich in culture, history, and romance that is located in the Veneto region, roughly 120 kilometers west of Venice. Its most well-known connection is to William Shakespeare's classic tragedy Romeo and Juliet, which has attracted numerous tourists to its streets who seek out the drama and passion captured in the play. But Verona is much more than merely the location of a great work of literature. Beautiful buildings, lively piazzas, Roman ruins, and a rich cultural legacy spanning more than two millennia can all be found in this city. A visit to Verona gives visitors to Venice the opportunity to see a different aspect of northern Italy, one that blends the grandeur of its historical significance with the beauty of a little city.

Verona is a great place for a day vacation because it's quick and convenient to get there from Venice. Since there are frequent and quick rail services connecting the two cities, taking the train is the most popular mode of transportation. Depending on whether you choose a high-speed or regional train, the trip takes roughly one to one and a half hours. Trains leave from Venice's Santa Lucia station and arrive at Verona Porta Nuova station. Faster and more comfortable, high-speed trains, like those run by Trenitalia or Italo, come at a slightly higher cost. Although they might take a little longer, regional trains are less expensive and still offer a pleasant ride. It's easy to begin exploring as soon as you get to Verona Porta Nuova because the city center is only a short walk or bus ride away.

Verona's association with Romeo and Juliet is among the first things that spring to mind when one thinks of the city. Even though Verona was never visited by Shakespeare, the city has accepted its role as the play's setting, and many of its sites are connected to the narrative. The most well-known of these is "Casa di Giulietta," or Juliet's House, which is located in the center of the city. The Capello family, whose name is believed to have inspired the Capulets in Shakespeare's play, is reported to have owned this 14th-century edifice. Visitors can witness the renowned balcony where Juliet is claimed to have stood during her amorous exchanges with Romeo, as well as a tiny courtyard with a bronze statue of Juliet. The spot has become a pilgrimage for Shakespeare aficionados and followers worldwide, even if the relationship to the play is primarily symbolic. Additionally, visitors can touch the statue of Juliet for good luck in love or write love notes on the courtyard's walls.

Another significant location associated with the Romeo and Juliet story is Romeo's House, also known as "Casa di Romeo." Although this medieval structure is not as well-known as Juliet's House, it is claimed to have been the residence of the Montecchi family, who are credited with serving as the inspiration for the Montagues in the play. Despite being closed to the public, the house is still worth viewing from the exterior because it offers insight into Verona's medieval past. Juliet's Tomb, which is housed in the old monastery of San Francesco al Corso, is another nearby attraction. The location is another well-liked venue for play fans, and legend has it that this is where Juliet was buried.

Verona is a city of extraordinary historical and architectural significance that extends beyond its literary associations. The Verona Arena, a Roman amphitheater from the first century AD, is one of its most recognizable landmarks. Even today, concerts, operas, and other acts take place in the surprisingly intact arena. It hosts the Verona Opera Festival in the summer, which draws top-notch actors and spectators from all over the world. You can explore the arena's historic stone seating and experience what it must have been like to see gladiatorial matches and other Roman spectacles, even if you are not there during the festival.

Piazza delle Erbe, Verona's central square and a center of activity, is another must-see destination. Historic structures encircle this bustling piazza, such as the medieval tower known as the Torre dei Lamberti, which provides expansive city views. Additionally, there is a daily market in the square where you may peruse local specialties, souvenirs, and fresh food. A smaller and more refined square that is frequently referred to as Verona's "living room" is Piazza dei Signori, right next door. This piazza, which is encircled by significant structures like the Loggia del Consiglio and the Palazzo della Ragione, is a wonderful spot to relax and take in the ambience while sipping coffee or gelato.

There are a number of stunning churches in Verona that are worth seeing for anyone interested in the city's religious history. One of the most significant is the Basilica of San Zeno Maggiore, which is regarded as a Romanesque architectural masterpiece. The inside of the church, which is devoted to Saint Zeno, Verona's patron saint, has exquisite frescoes and a bronze entrance with elaborate reliefs. Another noteworthy church is the Verona Cathedral, also known as the "Duomo di Verona," which features artwork by well-known artists like Titian and blends Gothic and Romanesque architectural styles. You will also come across Verona's numerous bridges, which cross the Adige River and contribute to the city's allure. The Ponte Pietra, a Roman bridge that has undergone multiple reconstructions over the ages, is the most well-known of these. Beautiful views of the river and the surrounding hills can be seen from this bridge, which is also a fantastic place to take pictures. Part of the Castelvecchio fortification, the Castelvecchio Bridge, also known as "Ponte Scaligero," is another noteworthy bridge. This medieval bridge is renowned for both its characteristic red brick design and its protective use throughout Verona's history.

Knowing a few essential Italian words will help you make the most of your trip to Verona. To get directions, for instance, you can say "Dov'è…?" (Where is…?) followed by the name of the location, like "Casa di Giulietta" or "Arena di Verona." To order food or beverages, you can say "Vorrei..." (I would like...) followed by the item you desire. Examples are "Vorrei un caffè" (I would like a coffee) and "Vorrei un gelato" (I would like a gelato). You may demonstrate your respect for the local language and culture and improve the quality of your interactions with them by using these easy phrases.

Practical advice: Since Verona's streets are cobblestoned and you will probably be walking a lot, it is a good idea to wear comfortable shoes when you visit. A Verona Card, which offers free or reduced admission to many of the city's famous sites, such as the Verona Arena, Juliet's House, and the Basilica of San Zeno, is a good option if you intend to visit several attractions. The card can be a reasonably priced option to explore the city's main attractions and is available for 24 or 48 hours.

Padua

A great option for a day excursion from Venice is Padua, also known as Padova in Italian, a city of great cultural, historical, and scientific value. With a history that stretches back to the Roman era, Padua is one of the oldest cities in Italy and is located just 40 kilometers west of Venice. This city offers tourists a singular fusion of art, history, and science by skillfully fusing its thriving present with its rich past. Padua is a place that attracts to a variety of interests because of its famous university, beautiful frescoes, and religious sites. A journey to Padua offers visitors to Venice the chance to experience the beauty and culture of northern Italy while exploring a more sedate, less crowded city. Although Padua's abundance of sights could easily fill many days, its small size and first-rate transit connections make it simple to visit in a single day.

The most popular way to get from Venice to Padua is by rail, which is easy and convenient. Frequent trains go between Padua's main train station and Venice's Santa Lucia station; high-speed trains can make the trip in as little as 25 minutes, while regional trains take about 40 minutes. Regional trains are less expensive and yet offer a decent journey, although high-speed trains run by Trenitalia or Italo are quicker and more comfortable. You can easily begin your investigation as soon as you get to Padua's train station because the city center is only a short tram ride or walk away. The majority of Padua's major attractions are accessible by foot, but the city's public transit system—which includes buses and trams—is effective and easy to use.

The Scrovegni Chapel, often called the Arena Chapel, is one of Padua's most well-known landmarks. One of the greatest works of Western art may be found in this tiny but remarkable chapel: a set of frescoes created by the well-known artist Giotto in the early 14th century. These frescoes, which are praised for their vibrant colors, profound emotional content, and creative use of perspective, feature scenes from the lives of Christ and the Virgin Mary as well as an incredible Last Judgment. Giotto's painting at the Scrovegni Chapel, which signifies the change from medieval to Renaissance styles, is regarded as a watershed in art history. Art enthusiasts should definitely visit the church, but it's vital to remember that access is tightly restricted in order to protect the fragile murals. Since only small groups are permitted entry and only stay for 15 minutes, visitors must purchase tickets in advance and arrive at a certain time. In order to assist regulate the atmosphere within the chapel, guests spend a few minutes in a climate-controlled area before entering. Even if the visit is short, it is definitely worth the effort to see Giotto's frescoes up close because it is an amazing experience.

One of the most significant pilgrimage sites in Italy is the Basilica of Saint Anthony, also known as the "Basilica di Sant'Antonio," which is another highlight of Padua. Saint Anthony of Padua, a cherished Catholic saint renowned for his teachings and miracles, is honored in this gorgeous church. The basilica's interior is embellished with exquisite altars, sculptures, and frescoes, and its architecture is a magnificent fusion of Byzantine, Gothic, and Romanesque styles. Many people visit Saint Anthony's shrine to pray or make offerings, and his grave is housed inside the basilica. Additionally, the basilica has a museum with saint-related artwork and religious relics on show. The bustling Piazza del Santo is located outside the basilica, where street sellers offer religious artifacts, souvenirs, and regional fare.

The University of Padua, one of the oldest and most prominent universities in Europe, was established in Padua in 1222. Galileo Galilei, who taught mathematics at the university in the early 17th century, is among the many famous people who have been linked to it. The university has a long tradition of intellectual distinction. The Anatomical Theatre, the first permanent edifice in the world dedicated to studying human anatomy, is one of the university's most well-known structures. Students used to congregate in this tiny, circular theater, which was constructed in 1594 and has high wooden levels where they could watch dissections. The university's museum now houses the Anatomical Theatre along with displays on the development of science and medicine. The Botanical Garden, also known as the "Orto Botanico," is another landmark of the university. It was founded in 1545 and is the oldest university botanical garden globally. The garden, which is a UNESCO World Heritage Site, has a modern greenhouse with interactive displays and a varied collection of plants, including rare and exotic species.

Prato della Valle in Padua is a must-see for everyone with an interest in architecture and history. One of the biggest elliptical squares in Europe, it is encircled by a canal that is lined with monuments of well-known historical personalities. The square is a well-liked meeting location for both locals and tourists, and it's a terrific place to unwind, take pictures, or have a picnic. The Basilica of Santa Giustina, a lesser-known but no less magnificent church, is located nearby and is well worth a visit. The interior of this basilica, which is devoted to the Christian martyr Saint Justina, is calm and adorned with exquisite artwork.

There are also a number of quaint piazzas, or squares, in Padua's ancient center that are ideal for exploration. Two of the city's liveliest squares, Piazza delle Erbe and Piazza della

Frutta, are the sites of daily markets where you can purchase handmade handicrafts, local specialties, and fresh fruit. Historic structures, such as the Palazzo della Ragione, a medieval town hall with an exquisitely frescoed interior, encircle these squares. Piazza dei Signori is another noteworthy square that is well-known for its vibrant cafes and exquisite architecture. Sitting in this square and taking in the city's atmosphere while sipping coffee or an aperitivo is a terrific idea.

Padua's charm and character are enhanced by the numerous bridges, canals, and winding streets you will come across while exploring the city. Because Padua was originally a major commerce hub that was connected to the Adriatic Sea via the Brenta River, the city's waterways serve as a reminder of its old Roman beginnings. An enjoyable approach to take in the city's distinct atmosphere is to stroll around the canals and cross the old bridges.

There are many delectable foods and specialties to sample in Padua for people who are interested in local cuisine. The city's robust, savory cuisine, which reflects the Veneto region's agricultural abundance, is well-known. Traditional foods to seek out include "risotto al radicchio," a creamy rice dish cooked with the area's renowned red radicchio, and "bigoli," a thick, spaghetti-like pasta dish frequently served with duck or anchovy sauce. Desserts like "torta pazientina," a layered cake composed with chocolate, custard, and almond paste, are another reason Padua is well-known. Try a glass of Prosecco or a regional red wine, like Valpolicella or Amarone, to go with your dinner.

Being able to speak a few simple Italian words will improve your trip to Padua. Saying "Dov'è…?" (Where is…?) and then the name of the location you're looking for, like "la Cappella degli Scrovegni" (the Scrovegni Chapel) or "la Basilica di Sant'Antonio" (the Basilica of Saint Anthony), is one way to get directions. You can say "Vorrei…" (I would like…) and then the item you want when ordering food or beverages. For instance, "Vorrei un bicchiere di vino" (I would like a glass of wine) or "Vorrei un caffè" (I would like a coffee). You may demonstrate your respect for the local language and culture and improve the quality of your interactions with them by using these easy phrases.

Palladian Architecture in Vicenza

Vicenza, a city in northern Italy's Veneto region, is a great option for a day trip from Venice because of its exceptional beauty and historical significance. Known as the "City of Palladio," Vicenza is praised for its magnificent architecture, much of which was created by Andrea Palladio, a well-known Renaissance architect. Because of the lasting impact his work in Vicenza had on the city, it was added to the UNESCO World Heritage list. For those who are interested in art, history, and architecture, Vicenza provides a singular chance to experience the elegance and charm of a little Italian city while simultaneously learning about the legacy of one of the most significant architects in history. Vicenza is a place that will enthrall and inspire tourists with its colorful piazzas, well-preserved architecture, and rich cultural history.

Due to excellent train connections, traveling from Venice to Vicenza is simple and convenient. The trip takes around 45 minutes on high-speed trains or about an hour on regional trains, and trains often leave from Venice's Santa Lucia station and arrive at Vicenza's main train station. Regional trains are less expensive and yet offer a decent journey, although high-speed trains run by Trenitalia or Italo are quicker and more comfortable. It's easy to begin sightseeing as soon as you get at Vicenza's train station because the city center is only a short stroll away. The majority of Vicenza's major attractions are accessible on foot due to the city's compact size and walkability, however buses and taxis are also available if necessary.

Since Vicenza is replete with examples of Andrea Palladio's architectural skill, the city is synonymous with his name. One of the finest Renaissance architects, Palladio lived in the 16th century, and his ideas have greatly influenced Western architecture. His use of classical elements influenced by ancient Roman architecture, as well as harmony and balance, are characteristics of his work. Palladio created a large number of buildings in Vicenza, including palaces, villas, and public buildings, many of which are still wonderfully intact today. One of the primary reasons to travel to Vicenza is to see these masterpieces, which provide an insight into the Renaissance's artistic and cultural accomplishments.

Palladio's Teatro Olimpico, which his student Vincenzo Scamozzi finished after his death, is one of Vicenza's most recognizable landmarks. The Teatro Olimpico is a Renaissance architectural marvel and the oldest indoor theater still standing in the world. It was constructed between 1580 and 1585. The stage, which is decorated with an intricate trompe-l'oeil background that gives the impression of a cityscape fading into the distance, is its most remarkable element. Palladio perfected the use of perspective, which he applied to many of his designs, to create an optical illusion. In addition, Palladio's love of ancient Roman architecture is evident in the theater's interior, which features classical columns, statues, and ornamental elements. To see the Teatro Olimpico as it was intended to be, visitors can watch a play or take a guided tour to learn about its history and design.

The Basilica Palladiana is a magnificent public structure in the center of Vicenza that is another must-see sight. The Basilica Palladiana, as its name suggests, is a municipal structure that was formerly a courthouse and marketplace rather than a church. Palladio added a stunning loggia with white marble arches and columns that encircle the building when he renovated it in the middle of the 16th century. One of the most identifiable emblems of Vicenza, the loggia is a prime illustration of Palladio's ability to blend classical features with avant-garde design. Today, the Basilica Palladiana has a museum, holds temporary shows, and has a rooftop terrace with sweeping city views. It is strongly advised to ascend to the terrace, which offers a distinctive view of the surrounding hills and Vicenza's ancient city.

Additionally, there are a number of palaces, or "palazzi," in Vicenza that were created by Palladio for affluent families in the Renaissance. Palladio's skill in designing graceful and well-balanced facades is evident in these palaces, which are dispersed across the city. The Civic Museum of Vicenza is located in Palazzo Chiericati, one of the most well-known. In addition to temporary exhibitions, this museum has a collection of decorative arts, paintings, and sculptures. Palazzo Barbaran da Porto, the location of the Palladio Museum, is another noteworthy palace. Andrea Palladio's life and work are honored at this museum, which also offers insightful information about his legacy and architectural philosophy. Models, sketches, and multimedia displays that bring Palladio's plans to life are available for visitors to examine.

Apart from its urban design, Vicenza is encircled by other Palladio-designed villas, many of which are located in the countryside not far from the city. These villas, which were constructed as rural homes for affluent families, are regarded as some of Palladio's most inventive and significant creations. Villa La Rotonda, sometimes called Villa Almerico Capra, is among the most well-known. With a central dome and four identical facades, each with a classical portico with columns, this house is well known for its symmetrical architecture. The villa's interior, which features lavishly furnished rooms and frescoes, is equally stunning. A highlight for anybody interested in Palladian architecture is the villa, which is privately held but open to the public on some days.

Located on a hill with a view of Vicenza, Villa Valmarana ai Nani is another noteworthy villa. The well-known artists Giambattista Tiepolo and his son Giandomenico painted the frescoes that are the focal point of this estate. The frescoes, which are regarded as some of the best examples of Venetian art from the 18th century, feature scenes from literature, mythology, and daily life. Exploring the villa's gardens is also worthwhile because they provide stunning views of the city below and the surrounding countryside.

You will also come across Vicenza's quaint piazzas, or squares, as you stroll throughout the city. These are ideal for unwinding and taking in the ambience. The central square of Vicenza's historic district is Piazza dei Signori. Important structures encircle it, such as the Basilica Palladiana and the Torre Bissara, a towering clock tower that provides yet another excellent location for city views. Piazza delle Erbe, a smaller plaza nearby, is the site of a daily market where you may purchase fresh fruit, regional delicacies, and trinkets. These squares offer a window into the everyday lives of the people who live in Vicenza and are active and dynamic.

Vicenza has a wide range of delectable foods and specialties to sample for people who are interested in local cuisine. The city's robust, savory cuisine, which reflects the Veneto region's agricultural abundance, is well-known. "baccalà alla vicentina," a slow-cooked salt fish dish eaten with polenta, is among the most well-known delicacies. The thick, spaghetti-like noodle known as "bigoli," which is frequently eaten with duck or anchovy sauce, is another regional delicacy. Wines from the neighboring Colli Berici hills are especially well-known in Vicenza. Try a glass of "Tai Rosso," a red wine that goes well with the food of the area.

Knowing a few simple Italian words will help you have a better time when you visit Vicenza. For instance, "Dov'è...?" (Where is...?) followed by the name of the location you're looking for, such "la Basilica Palladiana" (the Basilica Palladiana) or "il Teatro Olimpico" (the Teatro Olimpico), can be used to get directions. You can say "Vorrei..." (I would like...) and then the item you want when ordering food or beverages. "Vorrei un bicchiere di vino" (I would like a glass of wine) or "Vorrei un caffè" (I would like a coffee) are two examples. You may demonstrate your respect for the local language and culture and improve the quality of your interactions with them by using these easy phrases.

Vicenza is a city that provides tourists with a fulfilling and rich experience by fusing architecture, history, and art in a manner that is uncommon elsewhere. It is a must-see location for anybody interested in the Renaissance and the evolution of Western architecture because of its association with Andrea Palladio and his masterpieces. Vicenza is a city that will make an impression, from the Basilica Palladiana and the Teatro Olimpico to the exquisite palaces and villas. A day excursion to Vicenza offers visitors to Venice the chance to experience the beauty and culture of northern Italy while exploring a more sedate, less crowded city. Vicenza will enthrall and inspire you regardless of your interests—whether you are a history buff, art lover, or just trying to find a hidden treasure.

CHAPTER 9

USEFUL ADVICE FOR TRAVELERS

How to Keep Safe in Venice

For any visitor to this stunning and historic city, being safe in Venice is a top priority. Even while most people agree that Venice is one of the safest towns in Italy, if not all of Europe, it is still a major tourist destination, thus there are risks like pickpocketing and scams. You can make sure that your trip to Venice is secure, stress-free, and enjoyable by being aware of these possible problems and adopting a few easy safety measures. Traveling with peace of mind also requires knowing how to access emergency services and who to call in the event of a problem. Venice's distinctive design, with its canals, winding alleyways, and bridges, nevertheless poses certain difficulties for which tourists should be ready. You can confidently traverse the city and concentrate on taking in its beauty and charm if you are prepared and have the appropriate information.

Pickpocketing is one of the most frequent safety issues for visitors to Venice. Venice draws sizable crowds, much like many other well-known tourist locations, particularly at places like St. Mark's Square, the Rialto Bridge, and the Grand Canal. These busy areas are ideal targets for pickpockets, who frequently operate in groups and utilize deception tactics to take valuables like phones, wallets, and other items. It's critical to exercise caution and be alert to prevent becoming a victim of pickpocketing. Keep your possessions visible and close to hand at all times. Make use of a crossbody bag that you can wear in front of you or a zippered, safe bag. To make it more difficult for pickpockets to access your wallet, keep it in your front pocket instead than your back pocket and avoid carrying significant quantities of cash. Wearing your backpack on your chest in crowded places can help keep someone from opening it without your knowing.

Creating a distraction is another popular strategy employed by pickpockets. For instance, someone may ask for directions while an accomplice steals your possessions, bump into you, or pour anything on you. If someone comes up to you out of the blue or tries to talk to you in a way that doesn't seem right, be wary. Being particularly cautious when getting on or off vaporettos (water buses) is also a smart idea because pickpockets may take advantage of these crowded and moving situations. Follow your gut and leave if you see someone acting strangely or approaching too closely.

Visitors to Venice should be on the lookout for frequent scams in addition to pickpocketing. In one fraud, counterfeit products including watches, sunglasses, and designer handbags are sold by street vendors. Even though these things might look like a fantastic deal, buying fake goods is against the law in Italy, and you risk being fined if you are detected. Purchase only from reliable stores or approved providers to avoid this. Overcharging by cafes or restaurants, especially in tourist-heavy regions, is another trick to be wary of. Certain places might raise prices for tourists or add unstated levies. Always look at the menu before placing an order to avoid this, and inquire about any extra fees, like a "coperto" (cover charge) or service charge. You can ask, "Ci sono costi aggiuntivi?" (Are there more costs?) to get clarification if you're not sure.

Unofficial or unregistered tour guides may approach you around well-known sites and offer their services in another scam. These people might not be qualified or knowledgeable, and their excursions might not live up to your expectations in terms of quality or value. Ask your hotel for advice or make reservations for tours in advance through reliable businesses to prevent this. In a similar vein, be wary of those who offer to help you with your luggage or transportation because they can charge you an exorbitant amount. Seek out government employees or seek assistance at a tourist information center or your hotel if you need it.

Venice's distinct topography raises additional safety concerns. Since the city is located on a system of canals, many of its streets come to a sudden stop at the water's edge. Since most of the canals lack handrails, it's crucial to pay attention to your surroundings, particularly at night or in dimly lit regions. Avoid using your phone or other distractions when traversing the city's winding streets and bridges, and use caution when you're wandering close to the sea. Keep a tight watch on your kids if you're taking them along to make sure they stay safe around the canals. Certain parts of the city may flood during "acqua alta," or high tide, which makes walking more challenging. Use the higher walkways that are placed up in flooded areas and wear waterproof shoes or boots if you are visiting during this time.

Knowing who to call and how to get assistance is crucial in an emergency. In Italy, 112 is the universal emergency number that can be used to contact the police, fire department, or ambulance. You can also dial 118 to get an ambulance if you want medical assistance. The Ospedale Civile SS. Giovanni e Paolo, the city's primary hospital, is located in the Castello neighborhood and is one of several hospitals and clinics in Venice. You can visit a drugstore, or "farmacia," where employees can offer guidance and suggest over-the-counter medications, or ask your hotel for help if you need to see a doctor for a non-emergency matter. In Italy, pharmacies are identified by a green cross, and many of them are open around-the-clock or have extended hours.

Get in touch with your nation's embassy or consulate in Italy right away if you misplace your passport or other crucial documents. The staff can offer you other support or help you get a new paper. In the event that your passport is lost or stolen, it is advisable to have a photocopy with you and store it somewhere else from the original. A copy of the police report, which may be needed for insurance claims or for applying for a replacement passport, should be obtained after reporting the loss or theft to the local police.

Knowing a few simple phrases can aid travelers who don't know Italian when they need help or in an emergency. For instance, you could say "Ho bisogno di aiuto" (I need aid) or

"C'è un'emergenza" (There is an emergency) if you require assistance. You can say "Chiamate la polizia" (Call the police) if you need to call the police. You can say "Non mi sento bene" (I don't feel well) or "Ho bisogno di un dottore" (I need a doctor) if you're feeling ill. You can acquire the assistance you require and communicate with locals more easily if you know these basic terms.

Communication and Connectivity

Any journey must include connectivity and communication, and maintaining these while visiting Venice can significantly improve your experience. Having dependable internet access and communication tools is crucial, whether you need to use them to navigate the city's twisting streets and canals, remain in contact with loved ones, or post about your activities on social media. Wi-Fi networks, SIM cards, and mobile data plans are just a few of the alternatives available for staying connected in Venice, a well-liked tourist destination. Nonetheless, the city's distinct design and infrastructure can occasionally pose difficulties, so it's useful to know what options are available and how to take advantage of them while you're there.

Although Wi-Fi is readily available in Venice, the accessibility and quality of connections can differ according on where you are. The most practical way to access the internet while visiting is by using the free Wi-Fi that many hotels, guesthouses, and vacation rentals provide to their visitors. Some older buildings in Venice may have limited service, so it's a good idea to verify if Wi-Fi is included and available across the property before making your reservation. Hotel Wi-Fi networks are often password-protected; the password is either displayed in your room or given to you at check-in. Although hotel Wi-Fi is frequently dependable, connection reliability and speed can fluctuate, particularly during periods of high usage when many visitors are online.

Many cafes, restaurants, and bars in Venice provide free Wi-Fi to their patrons in addition to the Wi-Fi provided by hotels. If you need to check your email, find directions, or upload pictures while taking a break from touring, this can be a practical choice. The password, which is frequently given orally or printed on your receipt, may need to be asked for by the staff in order to access these networks. Remember that connection quality can vary and that certain businesses may have usage limitations or time limits. Carrying a portable charger or power bank is a smart idea if you intend to use public Wi-Fi because Wi-Fi can rapidly deplete your device's battery.

A local SIM card with a data package is a sensible choice for travelers who require more dependable and continuous internet connection. Prepaid SIM cards that can be used for calls, messages, and mobile data are available from TIM, Vodafone, WindTre, and Iliad, among other major mobile network providers in Italy. In Venice, these SIM cards are commonly accessible at train stations, airports, and cell phone stores. According to Italian legislation, you must present a legitimate form of identity, such as a passport, in order to buy a SIM card. You can select a prepaid plan that best fits your needs after buying a SIM card. Plans range from basic plans with restricted data to more extensive plans with unlimited data and international calling.

It may be less expensive to stay connected by using a local SIM card, particularly if you intend to use your phone a lot for social networking, streaming, or navigation. Before buying a SIM card, it's crucial to confirm that your phone is unlocked and compatible with European networks. Before your travel, you might need to get in touch with your provider to unlock your phone if it is locked to a particular carrier. Additionally, you might want to think about investing in a portable Wi-Fi hotspot, sometimes referred to as a pocket Wi-Fi device, if you are traveling with several devices, like a tablet or laptop. These gadgets, which are available for purchase or rental via mobile network providers or online, let you connect numerous devices to the internet with a single data plan.

Many foreign carriers have roaming packages that let you use your phone in Italy for a daily or monthly price if you would rather stick to your current mobile plan. These packages can be a practical choice if you don't want to convert to a local SIM card. They usually contain a certain quantity of data, calls, and texts. However, roaming fees can be costly, so it's crucial to confirm the costs and restrictions of your plan with your carrier before you travel. It's better to disable data roaming and use Wi-Fi whenever you can because using your phone overseas without a roaming package from your carrier can result in expensive data consumption fees.

It's crucial to consider internet security when keeping connected in Venice. Public Wi-Fi networks are susceptible to hacking and data theft, particularly if they are open and password-free. Avoid utilizing public Wi-Fi to access sensitive accounts, including email or online banking, in order to secure your personal data. If you must use these accounts, think about encrypting your connection and safeguarding your data with a virtual private network (VPN). For travelers who regularly use public Wi-Fi, a virtual private network (VPN) is a useful tool that establishes a private and secure connection between your device and the internet.

Staying connected in Venice requires knowing how to make both domestic and international calls in addition to having internet access. You can make calls within Italy by calling the local number directly if you are using a local SIM card. You must first dial the country code, then the area code, and then the phone number when making an international call. In the US, for instance, you would dial +1, then the area code and phone number to reach a number. You might need to activate international calling with your carrier before to your travel if you are using a SIM card from your home country. Because international calls can be costly, using internet-based communication apps like Zoom, Skype, or WhatsApp for video chats and conversations is frequently more economical. It can be beneficial for visitors who do not know Italian to learn a few fundamental terms pertaining to communication and networking. For instance, "Qual è la password del Wi-Fi?" (What is the Wi-Fi password?) can be used to request the password at a cafe or restaurant. "Vorrei una scheda SIM con un piano dati" (I would like a SIM card with a data plan) is a suitable phrase to use when buying a SIM card. You might ask, "Può aiutarmi a configurare il mio telefono?" (might you help me set up my phone?) if you need assistance configuring your phone or connecting to the internet. These short phrases can guarantee that you have the connectivity you require when traveling and facilitate communication with locals.

Maintaining communication is crucial for getting around Venice, keeping in touch with loved ones, and getting the most out of your trip. There are several options to fit your demands and budget, whether you decide to use an international roaming plan, buy a local SIM card, or rely on Wi-Fi. You may have a smooth and connected experience while soaking in Venice's beauty and charm by being aware of your options and taking precautions to safeguard your online security. You may concentrate on making treasured moments and sharing them with the world if you have the necessary equipment and are ready.

Venice's accessibility

For tourists with mobility issues, accessibility in Venice is crucial because of the city's distinctive design and historic infrastructure, which can pose major hurdles. Constructed on a system of islands connected by bridges, canals, and winding streets, Venice is a city unlike any other. Its design might be challenging for people with restricted mobility to navigate, despite its apparent beauty and charm. Nonetheless, recent years have seen improvements in accessibility, and visitors with mobility impairments can still take in Venice's delights with the right preparation and information. A seamless and pleasurable trip can be ensured by being aware of the services that are offered, the accessible routes, and helpful advice.

Venice's reliance on bridges to connect its numerous islands is a significant obstacle for those with mobility impairments. The majority of Venice's 400+ bridges have steps, which makes crossing them challenging for people in wheelchairs or with restricted mobility. Furthermore, the city's streets can be difficult to manage due to their cobblestones and frequent narrowness and unevenness. There are methods to see Venice with the least amount of hassle in spite of these barriers. The secret is to carefully plan your journeys and utilize the various possibilities that are offered.

The ACTV, Venice's public transportation system that runs the city's vaporettos (water buses), is one of the most crucial tools for tourists with mobility issues. One of the greatest ways to see Venice is in a vaporetto, which allows you to visit many of the city's major sights without having to cross bridges or negotiate challenging terrain. Wheelchair users may access most vaporetto stops since they have elevators or ramps. Not all stops are completely accessible, though, so it's a good idea to check the ACTV website or get in touch with customer care to find out about accessible routes and stops. The personnel on a vaporetto are often friendly and can help with boarding and disembarking if necessary. Additionally, it's important to remember that the ACTV provides cheaper tickets for travelers with impairments and their partners. Make sure to ask about this when buying tickets.

Venice has accessible water taxis in addition to vaporettos, which might be a practical choice for those seeking a more private form of transportation. Wheelchair users can reserve these water taxis in advance to guarantee availability, and they are furnished with ramps or lifts. Water taxis are a fantastic option for people who wish to escape congested public transit because they provide more comfort and flexibility than vaporettos, despite their higher cost. You can ask for help from your hotel or get in touch with one of the nearby water taxi businesses to reserve an accessible water taxi.

Some accessible pathways that are made to fit wheelchairs and other mobility devices are available for those who would rather tour Venice on foot. The most accessible routes are indicated by signage along these routes, which steer clear of step bridges and other obstructions. The area between St. Mark's Square, the center of Venice, and Piazzale Roma, the city's primary transportation hub, is among the easiest to get to. Ramps and other accessibility elements have been added to this route, making it simpler for passengers with mobility issues to navigate. Additionally, the Doge's Palace and St. Mark's Basilica, two of the city's most well-known sites, have installed elevators and ramps in an attempt to increase accessibility. It's crucial to remember that because of their age and architectural limitations, not all parts of these historic structures may be completely accessible.

The "Venezia Accessibile" program, which offers details on accessible routes, services, and attractions in Venice, is another useful tool for tourists with mobility issues. This project offers comprehensive information on the accessibility of important landmarks and museums, as well as an online map that shows accessible routes, vaporetto stops, and public restrooms. Travelers can avoid needless hassles and arrange their trip more efficiently by using this resource.

Your choice of lodging should be taken into account when organizing your vacation to Venice. Many of Venice's hotels are housed in old structures that might not have accessible doors or elevators. Make sure to ask about the property's accessibility features, such ramps, elevators, and accessible restrooms, when making your reservation. When booking, it's a good idea to inquire about any special accommodations that the hotel may have for visitors with disabilities. You can check online evaluations from other guests with mobility issues or get in touch with the hotel directly if you have any questions about its accessibility.

Other useful advice might help visitors with mobility issues make the most of their trip to Venice, beyond from transportation and lodging. For instance, it can be easier to maneuver through small streets and board vaporettos if you have a lightweight, collapsible wheelchair or other mobility aid with you. Wheelchair rentals are available from firms in Venice if you don't have your own mobility aid; they can be scheduled in advance. Even for people without mobility concerns, walking on the uneven streets and cobblestones can be exhausting, so it's crucial to wear supportive, comfortable shoes.

When asking for help or directions, it can be useful for tourists who do not speak Italian to know a few fundamental accessibility-related phrases. For instance, you can ask "È accessibile per sedie a rotelle?" (Is it wheelchair accessible?) if you need to know if a place is accessible. You might ask, "Può indicarmi un percorso accessibile?" (might you show me an accessible route?) if you require assistance identifying one. You can say "Ho bisogno di aiuto per salire" (I need help getting on) if you need assistance boarding a vaporetto or water taxi. These short phrases can help you get the help you need and facilitate communication with locals.

Knowing who to call and how to get assistance is crucial in an emergency. In Italy, 112 is the universal emergency number that can be used to contact the police, fire department, or ambulance. You can also dial 118 to get an ambulance if you want medical assistance. The Ospedale Civile SS. Giovanni e Paolo, the city's primary hospital, is located in the Castello neighborhood and is one of several hospitals and clinics in Venice. You can visit a drugstore, or "farmacia," where employees can offer guidance and suggest over-the-counter medications, or ask your hotel for help if you need to see a doctor for a non-emergency matter.

CONCLUSION

Venice is more than simply a city; it's a dream come true, where romance, art, and history all coexist together with the eternal elegance of its streets and the cadence of the canals. Venice provides a unique experience, as you have learned from this tour. Every area of this city has a tale to tell, from the majesty of the Doge's Palace and St. Mark's Basilica to the serene beauty of secret gardens and hidden squares. You can enjoy the rich flavors of Venetian food in a comfortable bacaro, float serenely along the canals in a gondola, or lose yourself in the lively energy of the Rialto Market. Venice has a way of winning your heart and leaving you with lifelong memories, whether you're touring top-notch museums, strolling through old neighborhoods, or just relaxing by the water and watching the gondolas pass by.

Venice's variety of experiences is what really sets it apart. You may take in the city's centuries-old architecture in the morning, have a leisurely lunch of fresh seafood by the lagoon, and watch the Grand Canal sunset at the end of the day. Whether you're a foodie, history buff, art enthusiast, or just someone who wants to experience the charm of a city unlike any other, there is something for every traveler to appreciate here. Venice encourages you to take your time, explore aimlessly, and enjoy the unplanned experiences that make traveling so fulfilling.

Now that you have seen everything Venice has to offer, it's time to move forward. Make your fantasy of traveling to Venice a reality by beginning your trip planning. You now have the knowledge and resources necessary to go around the city, find its hidden treasures, and make the most of your stay thanks to this book. You may now design an itinerary that suits your needs, whether it involves choosing where to stay, how to move about, or which sights to highlight. Don't hesitate; the trip of a lifetime is almost here, and Venice is calling.

As you get ready to go, keep in mind that Venice is an experience that will linger in your memory long after you've departed. The moments that will stick in your memory and serve as a reminder of the city's beauty are the sound of church bells resonating throughout the canals, the sight of sunshine dancing on the water, and the flavor of a well made risotto al nero di seppia. Every visitor to Venice is inspired, mesmerized, and changed by the city. It's a city that encourages you to view the world in a new way, to find beauty in every little thing, and to write tales that you will always treasure.

Prepare to experience one of the most remarkable locations on the planet by packing your baggage and bringing your sense of awe. Venice is eager to greet you with open arms and limitless opportunities. The memories you will create here will be really unforgettable, and your adventure is just getting started. You have the freedom to explore Venice and feel its enchantment for yourself.

Made in United States
North Haven, CT
05 May 2025